W9-ALX-275

Contents

Notes:

Evaluating Research in Academic Journals

A Practical Guide to Realistic Evaluation

Fred Pyrczak

California State University, Los Angeles

Pyrczak Publishing

P.O. Box 39731 • Los Angeles, CA 90039

Although the author and publisher have made every effort to ensure the accuracy and completeness of information contained in this book, we assume no responsibility for errors, inaccuracies, omissions, or any inconsistency herein. Any slights of people, places, or organizations are unintentional.

Editorial assistance provided by Brenda Koplin, Sharon Young, Elaine Fuess, Randall R. Bruce, and Cheryl Alcorn.

Cover design by Robert Kibler and Larry Nichols.

Printed in the United States of America.
10 9 8 7 6 5 4   DOC   06 05 04 03 02 01

ISBN 1-884585-19-1

Introduction

When students in the social and behavioral sciences take advanced courses in their major field of study, they are often required to read and evaluate original reports of research published as articles in academic journals. This book is designed as a guide for students who are first learning how to engage in this process.

Major Assumptions

First, it is assumed that the students using this book have limited knowledge of research methods even though they may have taken an introductory research methods course or may be using this book concurrently while taking such a course. Because of this assumption, technical terms and jargon such as "true experiment" are defined and explained when they are first used in this book.

Second, it is assumed that students have only a limited grasp of elementary statistics. Thus, the chapter on evaluating statistical reporting in research reports is confined to criteria such students can handle.

Finally, and perhaps most important, it is assumed that students with limited backgrounds in research methods and statistics can produce adequate evaluations of research reports—evaluations that get to the heart of important matters.

This book is *not* written for...

This book is not written for journal editors and members of their editorial review boards. Such professionals usually have had firsthand experience in conducting research and have taken advanced courses in research methods and statistics. Published evaluation criteria for use by these professionals are often terse, filled with jargon, and include many elements that cannot be fully comprehended without advanced training and experience. This book is aimed at a completely different audience: students who are just beginning to learn how to evaluate original reports of research.

Applying the Evaluation Questions in This Book

Chapters 2 through 12 are organized around evaluation questions that may be answered with a simple "yes" or "no," where a "yes" indicates that you judge a characteristic to be satisfactory. However, for evaluation questions that deal with complex issues, you may also want to rate each one using a scale from 1 to 5, where five is the highest rating. N/A (not applicable) may be used if you believe a characteristic does not apply, and I/I (insufficient information) may be used if you believe the research report does not contain sufficient information for you to make an informed judgment.

Evaluating Quantitative and Qualitative Research

Quantitative and qualitative research stem from different traditions and, thus, differ in purpose as well as methodology. Students who are not familiar with the distinctions between the two approaches are advised to read Appendix A, which presents a very brief overview of the differences, and Appendix B, which provides an overview of important issues in the evaluation of qualitative research. Most research methods textbooks present more detailed accounts of these matters.

While both approaches have long been used in the social and behavioral sciences, the quantitative approach has been dominant throughout the 1900s with the qualitative approach gaining in popularity near the end of the century. Still, the overwhelming majority of research reports in academic journals have a quantitative orientation, so the emphasis in this book is on evaluating this type of research. However, you will find that the vast majority of evaluation questions in this book apply to both types of research.

Using This Book in Classroom Settings

While this book may be used for self-study by interested individuals, it is designed primarily as a tool for use in classes in the social and behavioral sciences. It may be used in a variety of ways. For example, students may be assigned one or more research reports to read and evaluate for homework each week while using the evaluation guidelines and questions in this book. For the first homework session, students may be assigned an article and asked to apply the guidelines and evaluation questions in Chapters 1 through 3 only. During subsequent weeks, additional chapters and research reports may be assigned.

Some instructors may wish to have students evaluate one or more research reports as a term project with the students using this book independently to guide them in making their evaluations. Such students may be asked to answer or rate each evaluation question in this book as well as to write an explanation for each of their answers.

These as well as other uses of the book may be facilitated by photocopying Appendix C, Checklist of Evaluation Questions, for use with each research report that is evaluated. Limited permission to make such photocopies is given in the copyright notice on page *ii* of this book. Please read it carefully.

Chapter 1

Introduction to Evaluating Research Reports

Academic journals in the social and behavioral sciences abound with original reports of research. These are reports in which researchers describe how they identified a research problem, made relevant observations to gather data, and analyzed the data they collected. The reports usually conclude with a discussion of the results and their implications. This chapter provides an overview of some general characteristics of such research. Subsequent chapters present specific questions that should be applied in the evaluation of research reports.

✓ Guideline 1: Researchers very often examine only narrowly defined problems.

Comment: While researchers may be interested in broad problem areas such as violence against women or the mathematics achievement of middle school children, they very often examine only narrow aspects of such problems due to limited resources. Furthermore, they often examine them in such a way that the results can be easily reduced to numbers, further limiting their line of vision.[1] Example 1.1.1 illustrates how narrowly research problems are often defined. It deals with only one potential factor in violence against women, uses only college men as possible aggressors, and looks at only one type of aggressive behavior in a laboratory setting.

Example 1.1.1[2]
Brief synopsis of a study on violence against women, narrowly defined:

Misogynous rap music was played for 27 college males in a laboratory setting. The control group, consisting of another 27 college males, listened to neutral rap music. Then each male selected one of three videos to show a female college student: one that showed sexual violence against females, one that showed assaultive behavior toward females, and one that was

---

[1] Qualitative researchers (see Appendices A and B) generally take a broader view in defining a problem to be explored in research and are not constrained by the need to reduce the results to numbers and statistics.
[2] Barongan, C. & Hall, G. C. N. (1995). The influence of misogynous rap music on sexual aggression against women. *Psychology of Women Quarterly, 19,* 195–207.

neutral. Ninety-three percent of the males who listened to the neutral rap music selected the neutral video while only 70% of the males who listened to the misogynous rap music selected the neutral video.

Example 1.1.2 is another narrowly focused problem within a broad problem area.

Example 1.1.2[3]
Brief synopsis of a study on mathematics achievement, narrowly defined:

Researchers systematically examined the contents of three seventh-grade Japanese mathematics textbooks and four U.S. textbooks, looking at only a single lesson—a lesson on the addition and subtraction of signed whole numbers. The statistical results indicate that the Japanese books are superior to the U.S. ones in terms of several characteristics such as the percentage of space devoted to explanations of how to solve sample problems.

Because researchers often conduct their research on narrowly defined problems, an important task in the evaluation of research is to judge whether a researcher has defined the problem too narrowly to make an important contribution to the advancement of knowledge.

✓ Guideline 2: Researchers use less-than-perfect methods of observation.

Comment: In research, *observation* can take many forms from paper-and-pencil multiple-choice achievement tests to essay examinations, from administering a paper-and-pencil attitude scale with choices such as "strongly agree"–"strongly disagree" to conducting unstructured interviews to identify interviewees' attitudes. Of course, *observation* also includes direct observation of people interacting in their natural environments.

It is safe to assume that all methods of observation are flawed to some degree. To see why this is so, consider the matter of observing racial attitudes. Let's suppose a researcher decides to make direct observations of Whites and African Americans interacting (or not interacting) in the college cafeteria. Her observations will necessarily be limited to the types of behaviors typically exhibited in cafeteria settings—a weakness in her method of observation. In addition, she will be limited to observing only certain overt behaviors because it will be difficult for her, for example, to hear most of what is being said without

---

[3] Mayer, R. E., Sims, V., & Tajika, H. M. (1995). A comparison of how textbooks teach mathematical problem solving in Japan and the United States. *American Educational Research Journal, 32,* 443–460.

obtruding on the privacy of the students, and she will not be able to question them directly about their attitudes using only observation.

On the other hand, let's suppose that another researcher decides to measure racial attitudes by having students respond anonymously to racial statements by circling "agree" or "disagree" for each one. This researcher has an entirely different set of weaknesses in his observational system. First, there is the question of whether students will reveal their real attitudes on such a scale—even if it is anonymous. After all, most college students are aware that negative racial attitudes are severely frowned on in academic communities. Thus, some students might indicate what they believe to be socially desirable (i.e., socially "correct") rather than reveal their true attitudes. In addition, there is the problem of what specific racial statements to include on the scale. For example, if the statements are too harsh, they might not tap subtle, yet insidious, negative attitudes. Perhaps more important, the statements will be presented in isolation from a real-word context, making it easy for the students to misunderstand them or wonder about their full meaning.

We could continue looking at other ways to observe racial attitudes, each time finding potential problems. We could do the same thing for a host of variables other than racial attitudes. By now, however, this point is probably clear: There is *no perfect way to observe a given variable*. Instead, an evaluator must ask: *To what extent* is the observation method used in a particular study valid and reliable for the specific research purposes posed by the researcher. This matter will be considered in detail in Chapter 8.

✓ Guideline 3: Researchers usually use less-than-perfect samples.

Comment: Arguably, the most common sampling flaw in research reported in academic journals is the use of *samples of convenience* (i.e., samples that are readily accessible to the researchers). Most researchers are professors, and professors often use samples of college students—obviously as a matter of convenience. Another common flaw is that of relying on voluntary responses to mailed surveys, which are often quite low, with some researchers arguing that a response rate of about 60% or more is "acceptable." Other samples are flawed because researchers cannot identify and locate all members of a population (e.g., the homeless). Without being able to do this, it is impossible to draw a sample that a researcher can reasonably defend as being representative of the population.[4] In Chapters 6 and 7, specific criteria for evaluating samples are explored in detail.

---

[4] Qualitative researchers emphasize selecting a "purposive" sample—one that is likely to yield useful information—rather than a "representative" sample.

✓ Guideline 4: Even a seemingly straightforward analysis of data can produce misleading results.

Comment: Obviously, data-input and computational errors are a possible source of errors in results. Some commercial research firms have the data they collect entered independently by two or more data-entry clerks. A computer program checks to see whether the two sets of entries match perfectly—if not, there are errors, and the data need to be entered again. Oddly, taking such care in checking for mechanical errors in entering data is hardly ever mentioned in research reports published in academic journals.

In addition, there are alternative statistical methods for most problems, and different methods can yield different results.

Finally, even a nonstatistical analysis can be problematic. For instance, if two or more researchers review extensive transcripts of unstructured interviews, they might differ in their verbal summaries and interpretations of the interviewees' responses. Discrepancies such as these suggest that the results may be flawed—or, at least, subject to different interpretations.

These and other issues in data analysis are discussed in Chapter 10.

✓ Guideline 5: Original reports of research in journals often contain many details, which are of utmost importance when evaluating a report.

Comment: The old saying, "The devil is in the details," certainly applies here. Students who have relied exclusively on secondary sources for information about their major field of study may be surprised at the level of detail in research reports—typically much greater than even implied in secondary sources such as textbooks. Example 1.5.1 illustrates the level of detail that you can expect to find in many research reports published in academic journals.

Example 1.5.1[5]

An excerpt from an article illustrating the level of detail often reported in research reports in academic journals:

Our procedures closely followed those used in Olson's (1990) humor study. When the research participant arrived at the laboratory, the experiment was described as an investigation of the factors associated with perceptions of humor. They read joke monologues from two different books (one paired with a continuously looping laugh track and the other without the laugh track). The joke monologue paired with the laugh track was counterbalanced, as was the order of the laugh track's presentation, across participants.

---

[5] Graziano, W. G. & Bryant, W. H. M. (1998). Self-monitoring and the self-attribution of positive emotions. *Journal of Personality and Social Psychology, 74,* 250–261. Copyright © 1998 by the American Psychological Association.

As the experiment began, the experimenter placed one set of jokes on the table in front of the participant. The book (disguised with a plain, brown book jacket) from which the monologue was created was also placed in front of the participant. The participants read the joke monologues and rated the entire set for funniness (no individual joke ratings were obtained). The first set of jokes and book were removed from the desk, and the second monologue along with the book (also disguised with a plain, brown book jacket) from which it was created was placed in front of the participant, and the procedure was repeated.

Participants were told that the laugh track either increased their mirth or decreased their mirth, or they were given no special instructions. After reading the monologues, the participants evaluated, using a 5-point scale anchored at 1 (not at all) to 5 (very much so), how funny they thought the jokes were on the following questions: "How funny was the monologue?" "How much did you like the monologue?" "Would you consider telling some of the jokes in the monologue to a friend, assuming that you could remember them later?" Participants were also asked, "How much would you pay for a book containing the jokes used in the monologue ($0.00-$5.00)?"

Participants in the increased mirth condition were told the following:
It turns out that smiling and laughter are to a degree contagious. That is, people instinctively respond with smiling or laughter to other people's laughter. This tendency can be seen as early as very young infants, who will respond with a smile to their mother's smile. This is the reason that TV producers place laugh tracks over their comedy shows. Such laughter does, in fact, increase substantially smiling and laughter by the listeners. So keep this in mind—that is, your smiling and laughter were increased by the laugh track—while you complete these questions on how funny you thought the jokes were.

Those in the decreased mirth condition were told the following:
We are all familiar with laugh tracks or canned laughter on television shows. Is a laugh track really effective? That is, does it... (and so on).

Having detailed information on what was said and done to participants as well as on how they were observed makes it possible to make informed evaluations of research.

✓ **Guideline 6: Even highly detailed reports often lack information on matters that are potentially important for evaluating a research article.**

Comment: When you begin reading journal articles, you may be surprised to find that even major studies on very important issues are covered in rather brief reports. In most journals, research reports of more than about 15 pages are quite rare. Journal space is limited by economics—journals have limited readership and, thus, a limited paid circulation, and they seldom have advertisers. Given this situation, researchers must judiciously choose the details they will report. Sometimes, they may omit information that readers deem important.

Often omitted details cause problems for evaluators. For example, it is common for researchers to describe in general terms the attitude scales they used without reporting the exact wording of the items on the scales. Yet, there is considerable research indicating that how items are worded can affect the results obtained by using them.[6] Of course, judgments about the adequacy of the items cannot be made in their absence.

As you apply the evaluation questions throughout this book while evaluating research published in academic journals, you may be surprised how often you must answer "insufficient information to make a judgment." If this is your response to many of the questions as you apply them to a given report, you may well conclude that the report is too lacking in details to make an important contribution to science.

✓ Guideline 7: Some research reports published in academic journals are methodologically very weak.

Comment: With many hundreds of editors of and contributors to academic journals, it should not surprise you that published research reports vary in quality with some being very weak in terms of their research methodology.[7]

Undoubtedly, some weak reports simply slip past careless editors. More often, an editor may make a deliberate decision to publish a weak report because the problem it explores is likely to be of current interest to his or her readers. Let's consider one example to illustrate the justification for such decisions: the issue of charter schools, which is currently a topic of great interest in education. Briefly, a charter school is one that is allowed to bypass many of the government dictates on how schools must operate, giving parents, teachers, and principals freedom to collaborate in order to establish processes that may deviate from the norm, presumably in the best interests of the students. Let's suppose that a researcher wants to compare the progress of students enrolled in charter schools with those in schools that do not have charter status. He or she has this problem: Students are not assigned to schools at random (like drawing names out of a hat). Therefore, the students in the two types of schools may initially differ substantially in terms of a number of characteristics that may affect their educational progress such as their socioeconomic backgrounds, their parents' involvement in the schools, their motivation to learn, and so on. In other words, differences in students' progress between the two types of schools might be the result of (a) initial differences between the two groups of students or (b) differences in the programs they receive (charter vs. noncharter

---

[6] This statement appears in each issue of *The Gallup Poll Monthly*: "In addition to sampling error, readers should bear in mind that question wording…can introduce additional systematic error or 'bias' into the results of opinion polls." Accordingly, this journal reports the exact wording of the questions they use in their polls. Other researchers cannot always do this because the measures they use may be too long to include in the report or may be copyrighted by publishers who do not want the items released to the public.

[7] Many journals are "refereed." This means that the editor has experts act as referees by evaluating each paper submitted for possible publication. These experts make their judgments without knowing the identification of the researcher who submitted the paper, and the editor uses their input in deciding which papers to publish as journal articles.

programs).[8] The editor of an education journal might reasonably conclude that publishing studies with this weakness is better than publishing no studies on this important educational reform.

Sometimes studies with very serious methodological problems are labeled as *pilot studies*, either in their titles or introductions to the research reports. A pilot study is a preliminary study that allows a researcher to try out new methods and procedures for conducting research with small samples, which may be refined in subsequent studies. Publication of pilot studies, despite their limited samples and other potential weaknesses, is justified on the basis that they may point other researchers in the direction of promising new leads.

✓ Guideline 8: No research report provides "proof."

Comment: If you have been following closely in this chapter, you will not be surprised by this guideline. Conducting research is fraught with pitfalls, and any one study may have very misleading results. This is not to suggest, however, that research should be abandoned as a method for advancing knowledge. Instead, the solution is, in part, to evaluate individual research reports carefully to identify those that are most likely to provide sound results. The second part of the solution is to look across studies on the same research problem. If different researchers using different research methods with different types of strengths and weaknesses all reach similar conclusions, we can say that we have *considerable confidence* in the conclusions. On the other hand, to the extent that the body of research on a topic yields mixed results, we will lower our degree of confidence. For example, if the studies that we judge individually to be strong all point in the same direction while weaker ones point in a different direction, we might say that we have *some confidence* in the conclusion suggested by the stronger studies.

A caveat: If a speaker says "research *proves* that blah blah blah," you will know that you are receiving information from a naïve person. Beware. Read the research on the topic for yourself if the matter is important to you. Another statement that is the sign of a naïve or careless speaker is "such and such *a study shows* that blah blah blah." Listeners are likely to infer from such a statement that "shows" means "proves" and that a single study can prove something. Professionals who have studied and carefully considered research methods and statistics will hedge their remarks, using statements such as "such and such a study *suggests* that...," "an important study *provides strong*

---

[8] Statistical methods may be used to take account of initial differences between students in the two types of schools, but these methods depend on the ability to identify and validly measure all the important differences that may affect the outcomes of the study. Even if a researcher makes a strong argument that this has been done in a particular study, the outcome is not as satisfactory as having assigned students at random to the two types of schools.

evidence that…," or "a pilot study provides *preliminary information indicating* that…."

✓ Guideline 9: To become an expert on a topic, you must become an expert at evaluating original reports of research.

Comment: An expert is someone who knows not only broad generalizations about a topic but also the nuances of the research that underlie them, that is, he or she knows the particular strengths and weaknesses of the major studies used to arrive at the generalizations. For example, suppose a school board hires an expert on reading instruction to assist with a decision regarding the emphasis to place on the phonics and the whole language methods of reading instruction.[9] Members of the board should expect the expert to be familiar with the range of research on this controversy as well as the quality of individual studies on the topic. Such an expert should be able to make recommendations based on generalizations reached by considering the *quality of the evidence* found in research reports. He or she should be able to point out what is likely to be true and untrue based on careful evaluations of the reports.

As you begin taking upper-division courses, your goal should be to become an expert on the topics central to the profession you are preparing for, and you can do this only by carefully evaluating the research on these topics. At the graduate level, you will not only want to refine your expertise but also make creative contributions by conducting new research. Careful and insightful review and evaluation of existing research will help you become a better researcher because you will learn from the mistakes and triumphs of other researchers. Immersing yourself in and evaluating published research, much of which is highly creative, is likely to spark your own creativity.

Exercise for Chapter 1

Part A: Review

Directions: The nine guidelines discussed in this chapter are repeated below. For each one, indicate the extent to which you were already familiar with it before reading this chapter. Use a scale from 1 (not at all familiar) to 5 (very familiar).

---

[9] As you may know, phonics stresses sounding out letters and parts of words. Whole language emphasizes providing a rich language environment (e.g., many complete books, numerous verbal experiences such as reading books to students) that stimulates children to learn to read.

Guideline 1: Researchers very often examine only narrowly defined problems.

Familiarity rating: 5   4   3   2   1

Guideline 2: Researchers use less-than-perfect methods of observation.

Familiarity rating: 5   4   3   2   1

Guideline 3: Researchers usually use less-than-perfect samples.

Familiarity rating: 5   4   3   2   1

Guideline 4: Even a seemingly straightforward analysis of data can produce misleading results.

Familiarity rating: 5   4   3   2   1

Guideline 5: Original reports of research in journals often contain many details, which are of utmost importance when evaluating a report.

Familiarity rating: 5   4   3   2   1

Guideline 6: Even highly detailed reports often lack information on matters that are potentially important for evaluating a research article.

Familiarity rating: 5   4   3   2   1

Guideline 7: Some research reports published in academic journals are methodologically very weak.

Familiarity rating: 5   4   3   2   1

Guideline 8: No research report provides "proof."

Familiarity rating: 5   4   3   2   1

Guideline 9: To become an expert on a topic, you must become an expert at evaluating original reports of research.

Familiarity rating: 5   4   3   2   1

Part B: Application

Directions: Read a report of research published in an academic journal and respond to the following questions. The report may be one that you select or one that is assigned by your instructor. If you are using this book without any prior training in research methods, do the best you can in answering the questions at this point. As you work through this book, your evaluations will become increasingly sophisticated.

1. How narrowly is the research problem defined? In your opinion, is it too narrow? Is it too broad? Explain.

2. Are there any obvious flaws or weaknesses in the researcher's methods of observation? Explain. (Note: Observation or measurement is often described under the subheading "Instrumentation.")

3. Are there any obvious sampling flaws? Explain.

4. Was the analysis statistical or nonstatistical? Was the description of the results easy to understand? Explain.

5. Were the descriptions of procedures and methods of observation sufficiently detailed? Were any important details missing? Explain.

6. Overall, was the research obviously very weak? If yes, briefly describe its weaknesses and speculate on why it was published despite them.

7. Does the researcher imply that his or her research *proves* something? Do you believe that it proves something? Explain.

Chapter 2

Evaluating Titles

The primary function of titles is to help readers identify journal articles of interest to them. You should make a preliminary evaluation of a title when you first encounter it. After reading the article, reevaluate the title.

The evaluation questions are stated as "yes–no" questions where a "yes" indicates that you judge the characteristic of a title to be satisfactory. You may also want to rate each characteristic using a scale from 1 to 5, where 5 is the highest rating. N/A (not applicable) and I/I (insufficient information to make a judgment) may also be used.

___ 1. Is the title sufficiently specific?

Comment: On any major topic in the social and behavioral sciences, there are likely to be many hundreds of research reports published in academic journals. In order to help potential readers locate those that are most relevant to their needs, researchers should use titles that are sufficiently specific so that each article can be differentiated from the others in terms of their content and focus.

Consider the topic of depression, which has been extensively investigated. The title in Example 2.1.1 is insufficiently specific. Contrast it with the titles in Example 2.1.2, which contains information that differentiates each one from the others.

Example 2.1.1
A title that is insufficiently specific:

An Investigation of Adolescent Depression and Its Implications

Example 2.1.2
Three titles that are more specific than the one in Example 2.1.1:

Gender Differences in the Expression of Depression by Early Adolescent Children of Alcoholics

The Impact of Social Support on the Severity of Depression Among Gay and Lesbian Adolescents

The Effectiveness of Cognitive Therapy in the Treatment of Adolescent Students with Severe Depression

___ 2. Does the title indicate the nature of the research without describing the results?

Comment: It is usually inappropriate for a title to describe the results of a research project. Use of observational methods, which are inherently flawed as noted in Chapter 1, often raises more questions than answers. In addition, the results are often subject to more than one interpretation. Consider Example 2.2.1, which undoubtedly oversimplifies the results of the study. An accounting of the results should address issues such as: What type of social support (e.g., parental support, peer support, and so on) is effective? How strong does it need to be to lessen the depression? By how much is depression lessened by strong social support? and so on. Because it is usually impossible to state results accurately and unambiguously in a short title, results ordinarily should *not* be stated at all as illustrated in Example 2.2.2.

Example 2.2.1
A title that inappropriately describes results:

Strong Social Support Lessens Depression Among Gay and Lesbian Adolescents

Example 2.2.2
A title that appropriately does not describe results:

The Relationship Between Social Support and Depression Among Gay and Lesbian Adolescents

___ 3. Has the author avoided using a "yes–no" question as a title?

Comment: Because research rarely yields simple, definitive answers, it is seldom appropriate to use a title that poses a simple "yes–no" question. For instance, Example 2.3.1 implies that there is a simple answer to the question it poses. However, a study on this topic undoubtedly explores *the extent to which boys and girls differ in the use of various mathematical strategies*—a much more interesting topic than suggested by the title. Example 2.3.2 is cast as a statement and is more appropriate as the title of a research report for publication in an academic journal.

Example 2.3.1
A title that inappropriately poses a "yes–no" question:

Do First-Grade Boys and Girls Differ in Their Use of Mathematical Problem-Solving Strategies?

Example 2.3.2
A more appropriate title than the one in Example 2.3.1:

Gender Differences in First-Grade Mathematics Problem-Solving Strategies

____ 4. If there is a main title and a subtitle, do both provide important information about the research?

Comment: Failure on this evaluation question often results from an author using a "clever" main title that is vague and following it up with a subtitle that identifies the specific contents of the research report. Example 2.4.1 illustrates this problem. As you can see, the main title is vague and fails to impart important information. In fact, it could apply to thousands of studies in which researchers find that various combinations of variables (the parts) contribute to our understanding of a complex whole.

Example 2.4.1
A two-part title with a vague main title:

The Whole is Greater Than the Sum of the Parts: The Relationship Between Playing with Pets and Longevity Among the Elderly

Example 2.4.2 is also deficient because the main title is vague.

Example 2.4.2
A two-part title with a vague main title:

The Other Side of the Story: The Relationship Between Social Class and Mothers' Involvement in Their Childrens' Schooling

In contrast to the above two examples, Example 2.4.3 has a main title and a subtitle, both of which contain specific information about a research study.

Example 2.4.3
A two-part title in which both parts provide important information:

Attachment to Parents and Emotional Well-Being: A Comparison of African American and White Adolescents

The title in Example 2.4.3 could be rewritten as a single statement without a subtitle, as illustrated in Example 2.4.4.

Example 2.4.4

A rewritten version of Example 2.4.3:

A Comparison of the Emotional Well-Being and Attachment to Parents of African American and White Adolescents

Do you think that Example 2.4.3 or 2.4.4 is a more effective and efficient title? The answer is probably arguable. Thus, the evaluation question we are considering here is neutral on whether a title should be broken into a main title and subtitle. Rather, it suggests that if it is broken into two parts, both parts should provide important information specific to the research being reported.

___ 5. Are the primary variables referred to in the title?

Comment: Variables are the characteristics of the participants that varied or differed from one participant to another. In Examples 2.4.3 and 2.4.4 above, the variables are (1) attachment to parents, (2) emotional well-being, (3) and race. That is, the participants could *vary* on attachment to parents with some adolescents having more of it and some having less. Likewise, they could vary on emotional well-being and race.

Note that "adolescents" is *not* a variable because the title clearly suggests that only young adolescents were studied. In other words, "adolescents" is a *common trait* of all the participants—a trait that helps to identify them as the population of interest. (The matter of identifying the population in a title is discussed under the next evaluation question.)

When researchers study many specific variables in a given study, they appropriately may refer to the *type(s)* of variable(s) in their titles rather than naming each one individually. For example, suppose a researcher administered a major achievement test battery that measures spelling ability, reading comprehension, vocabulary knowledge, mathematical problem-solving skills, and so on. Naming all these variables would create a title that is much too long. Instead, the researcher could refer to the collection of variables as *academic achievement*, which is done in Example 2.5.1.

Example 2.5.1

A title in which types of variables (achievement variables) are referred to:

The Relationship Between Parental Involvement in Schooling and Academic Achievement in the Middle Grades

___ 6. Does the title indicate what types of people participated?

Comment: Research methods textbooks suggest that researchers should name the population of interest in their reports. It follows that it is often desirable to include a reference to the population in the title. From the title in Example 2.6.1, it would be reasonable to infer that the population of interest consists of graduate students who are taking a statistics class. This would certainly be of interest to someone who is searching through a listing of the hundreds of articles on cooperative learning. Knowing that it deals with this population might rule it out as an article of interest to someone who is trying to locate research on the use of cooperative learning in teaching beginning reading.

Example 2.6.1
A title in which the type of participants is mentioned:

Effects of Cooperative and Individual Learning in a Graduate Level Statistics Class

Example 2.6.2 also names an important characteristic of the research participants—the fact that they are hearing-impaired children.

Example 2.6.2
A title in which the type of participants is mentioned:

Academic Achievement and Academic Self-Concept in Hearing-Impaired Children

Note that many researchers do not explicitly name a population of interest in their research reports. Instead, they describe the demographics of the sample they used with statements such as "The participants were 100 undergraduates enrolled in a psychology class who participated in the research for course credit. Fifty-five percent were male. A majority (70%) were White, 15% were African American, 4% were Asian American...." As you read the research report, you may well reach the conclusion that the researcher has no special interest in undergraduates enrolled in an introductory psychology course *per se*; rather, you may decide that the researcher is interested in research questions that may have broad implications for people from many strata in life and happened to use undergraduates simply because they were readily accessible. Likewise, he or she may have no particular interest in racial/ethnic differences but happened to use a racially/ethnically diverse sample merely because it was convenient to do so. In such a case, it might be *inappropriate* to include mention of these characteristics of the participants in the title. Thus, you will sometimes need to make a judgment call as to whether the characteristics of the participants should be mentioned in the title of a research report.

___ 7. If the title implies causality, does the method of research justify it?

Comment: Example 2.7.1 implies that causal relationships have been examined because it contains the word *effects*. In fact, this is a keyword frequently used by researchers in their titles to indicate that they have explored causality in their studies. A common method to examine causal relations is to conduct an *experiment*. As you may know, an experiment is a study in which different groups of participants are given different treatments (such as giving one group computer-assisted instruction while using a more traditional method to teach another group). The researcher compares the outcomes obtained by applying the various treatments.[1] When such a study is conducted, the use of the word "effects" in the title is justified.[2]

Example 2.7.1
A title in which causality is implied by the word "effects":

The Effects of Computer-Assisted Instruction in Mathematics on Students' Achievement and Attitudes

The title in Example 2.7.2 also suggests that the researcher examined a causal relationship because of the inclusion of the word *effects*. Note that in this case, however, the researcher probably did *not* investigate the relationship using an experiment because it would be unethical/illegal to manipulate breakfast as an independent variable (i.e., we would not want to assign some students to receive breakfast while denying it to others for the purposes of an experiment).

Example 2.7.2
A title in which causality is implied by the word "effects":

The Effects of Breakfast on Student Achievement in the Primary Grades

When it is not possible to conduct an experiment on a causal issue, researchers often conduct what are called *ex post facto* (i.e., *causal comparative*) studies. In these studies, researchers identify students who are different on some outcome (such as students who are high and low in achievement in the primary grades) but who are the same on demographics and other potentially influential variables (such as parents' highest level of

---

[1] Experiments can also be conducted by treating a given person or group differently *at different points in time*. For example, we might praise a child for staying in his or her seat in the classroom on some days and not praise him or her on others while comparing the child's seat-staying behavior under the two conditions.

[2] The evaluation of experiments is considered in Chapter 9. Note that the evaluation question merely asks if there is a basis for suggesting causality in the title (i.e., reference to causality may be justified even if the research methods are subject to criticism as long as the author attempted to use methods appropriate for examining causality). It does not ask you to judge the quality of the experiment or ex post facto study.

education, parental income, quality of the schools the children attend, and so on). Comparing the two groups' breakfast eating habits might yield some useful information on whether eating breakfast *affects*[3] students' achievement because the two groups are similar on other variables that might account for differences in achievement (e.g., their parents' level of education is similar). If a researcher has conducted such a study, the use of the word *effects* in the title is justified.

Note that simply examining a relationship without controlling for potentially confounding variables does *not* justify a reference to causality in the title. For example, if a researcher merely compared the achievement of children who regularly eat breakfast with those who do not without controlling for other explanatory variables, a causal conclusion (and, hence, a title suggesting it) usually cannot be justified.

Also note that synonyms for *effect* are *influence* and *impact*. Their use should also usually be restricted to use in titles of studies that are either experiments or ex post facto studies.

___ **8. Has the author avoided using jargon and acronyms that might be unknown to his or her audience?**

Comment: Professionals in all fields use jargon and acronyms (shorthands for words, usually spelled in all capital letters) for efficient and accurate communication with their peers. However, their use in titles of research reports is inappropriate unless the researchers are writing exclusively for such peers. Consider Example 2.8.1. If ACOA is likely to be well-known to all the readers of the journal in which this title appeared, its use is appropriate; otherwise, it should be spelled out or its meaning paraphrased. As you can see, it is difficult to make this judgment without being very familiar with the journal and its audience. Nevertheless, if you are reading an article on a topic on which you have already read extensively and encounter an acronym that you do not understand in the title of an article, its use is probably inappropriate.[4]

Example 2.8.1
A title with an acronym that is not spelled out:

The Interaction Effects of Gender with Recovering ACOA Alcoholics and non-ACOA Alcoholics[5]

---

[3] Note that when referring to an outcome caused by some agent, the word is spelled *effects* (i.e., it is a noun). As a verb meaning "to influence," the word is spelled *affects*.
[4] As you may know, ACOA stands for Adult Children of Alcoholics.
[5] Sandoz, C. J. (1996). *Alcoholism Treatment Quarterly, 14,* 67–77.

____ 9. Overall, is the title effective and appropriate?

Comment: Rate this evaluation question after considering your answers to the earlier ones in this chapter and any additional considerations and concerns you may have. Be prepared to rewrite the titles of research reports to which you assign low ratings.

Exercise for Chapter 2

Directions: Evaluate each of the following titles to the extent that it is possible to do so without reading the complete research reports. The references for the titles are given below; all are from journals that are widely available in large academic libraries, making it possible for you to consult the complete articles if they are assigned by your instructor. More definitive application of the evaluation criteria for titles is possible by reading complete articles and then evaluating their titles.

1. Taking the Sting Out of the Whip: Reactions to Consistent Punishment for Unethical Behavior[6]

2. Problem-Based Learning: A Coat of Many Colours[7]

3. Are Adult Children of Dysfunctional Families with Alcoholism Different from Adult Children of Dysfunctional Families without Alcoholism? A Look at Committed, Intimate Relationships[8]

4. "We Never Talk About That": A Comparison of Cross-Sex Friendships and Dating Relationships on Uncertainty and Topic Avoidance[9]

5. Legal Gambling and Crime[10]

6. Testimony in a Social Setting[11]

7. The Masculine Image of Careers in Science and Technology: Fact or Fantasy?[12]

---

[6] Bennett, R. J. (1998). *Journal of Experimental Psychology: Applied, 4,* 248–262.

[7] Lloyd-Jones, G., Margetson, D., & Bligh, J. G. (1998). *Medical Education, 32,* 492–494.

[8] Harrington, C. & Metzler, A. E. (1997). *Journal of Counseling Psychology, 44,* 102–107.

[9] Afifi, W. A. & Burgoon, J. K. (1998). *Personal Relationships, 5,* 255–272.

[10] Lester, D. (1998). *Psychological Reports, 83,* 382.

[11] Vicario, G. B. & Tomat, L. (1998). *Perceptual and Motor Skills,* 1075–1082.

[12] Lightbody, P. & Durndell, A. (1996). *British Journal of Educational Psychology, 66,* 231–246.

8. Are We Missing the Forest for the Trees? Considering the Social Context of School Violence[13]

9. Today's Husband More Involved in Household Duties than Post-WWII Generation[14]

10. Effects of a Prepaid Nonmonetary Incentive on Response Rates and Response Quality in a Face-to-Face Survey[15]

11. Lower-Fat Menu Items in Restaurants Satisfy Customers[16]

12. The Changes in the Social Class Distribution of Moderate and High Alcohol Consumption and of Alcohol-Related Disabilities Over Time in Stockholm County and in Sweden[17]

13. Comorbidity Between DSM-IV Alcohol and Drug Use Disorders: Results from the National Longitudinal Alcohol Epidemiologic Survey[18]

14. Correlation Between History of Contact with People Living with HIV/AIDS (PWAs) and Tolerant Attitudes Toward HIV/AIDS and PWAs in Rural Thailand[19]

---

[13] Baker, J. A. (1998). *Journal of School Psychology, 36*, 29–44.

[14] Moore, D. W. (1997). *The Gallup Poll Monthly*, No. 378, March, 8–12 & 54.

[15] Willimack, D. K., Schuman, H., Pennell, B., & Leplowski, J. M. (1995). *Public Opinion Quarterly, 59*, 78–92.

[16] Fitzpatrick, M. P., Chapman, G. E., & Barr, S. I. (1997). *Journal of the American Dietetic Association, 97*, 510–514.

[17] Romelsjoe, A. & Lundberg, M. (1996). *Addiction, 91*, 1307–1323.

[18] Grant, B. F. & Pickering, R. P. (1996). *Alcohol Health & Research World, 20*, 67–72.

[19] Takai, A., Wongkhomthong, S., Akabayashi, A., Kai, I., Ohi, G., & Naka, K. (1998). *International Journal of STD & AIDS, 9*, 482–484.

Notes:

Chapter 3

Evaluating Abstracts

An abstract is a summary of a research report that appears just below the title and the name(s) of the author(s). Like the title, it helps readers identify articles of interest. This function of abstracts is so important that the major computerized databases in the social and behavioral sciences provide abstracts as well as the titles of the articles they index.

Many journals have a policy on the maximum length of abstracts. It is common to allow a maximum of about 100 to 250 words.[1] When evaluating them, you will need to make subjective decisions about how much weight should be given to the various elements that might be included in an abstract, given that its length is severely restricted.

You should make a preliminary evaluation of an abstract when you first encounter it. After reading the article, reevaluate it. The following evaluation questions are stated as "yes–no" questions where a "yes" indicates that you judge the characteristic to be satisfactory. You may also want to rate each characteristic using a scale from 1 to 5, where 5 is the highest rating. N/A (not applicable) and I/I (insufficient information to make a judgment) may also be used.

____ 1. Is the purpose of the study referred to or at least clearly implied?

Comment: Many writers begin their abstracts with a brief statement of the purpose of their research. Examples 3.1.1 and 3.1.2 show the beginnings of abstracts in which this was done. Note that even though the word "purpose" is not used in Example 3.1.2, it is easy to infer that the purpose was to assess the impact of a drug education course.

---

[1] The *Publication Manual of the American Psychological Association* suggests that an abstract should summarize a research report in 100 to 120 words. A small number of journals require much more extensive abstracts broken down with subheadings such as *Background, Purpose, Method,* and so on. These might take up to half a page. Although they are called abstracts, they are similar to executive summaries used in business, which allow busy executives to keep abreast of large numbers of reports coming across their desks without having to read each one in full. Most of the journals that require long, detailed abstracts are in the fields of business and health care.

Example 3.1.1[2]

Beginning of an abstract that describes the purpose of the study:

The purpose of this research was to explore whether there are significant differences in White racial identity attitudes between White students who have lived with Black roommates and those who lack such interaction. The….

Example 3.1.2[3]

Beginning of an abstract that implies the purpose of the study:

Assessed the impact that a drug education course had on motives, consequences, attitudes, and perceptions regarding alcohol use in 12 university students….

Beginning an abstract with an explicit statement of the research purpose is not necessary as long as the purpose can be inferred from the title and other information contained in the abstract. Consider the title and beginning of the abstract shown in Example 3.1.3. Taken in their entirety, the title and abstract together make it easy to infer that the purpose is to explore the conditions under which students will yield to peer pressure to ride with an intoxicated driver.[4]

Example 3.1.3[5]

Title of an article:

The Role of Peer Conformity in the Decision to Ride with an Intoxicated Driver

The associated abstract:

Forty university students participated in a study in which they were faced with the decision of whether or not to enter an automobile with an apparently intoxicated driver. Participants were randomly assigned to one of four conditions: Driver with one beer, intoxicated driver, intoxicated driver and confederate[6] who enters the car, and intoxicated driver and

---

[2] Newswanger, J. F. (1996). The relationship between White racial identity attitudes and the experience of having a Black college roommate. *Journal of College Student Development, 37,* 536-542.

[3] Duitsman, D. M. & Cychosz, C. M. (1997). The efficacy of a university drug education course on factors that influence alcohol use. *Journal of Drug Education, 27,* 223-229.

[4] This point runs counter to a principle that you may have learned in a freshman composition course. Normally, a paper or article should be able to stand on its own without reference to its title. However, given that both must be brief in a research report and that someone evaluating a report would undoubtedly read both, this principle of composition is not applied here.

[5] Powell, J. L. & Drucker, A. D. (1997). The role of peer conformity in the decision to ride with an intoxicated driver. *Journal of Alcohol and Drug Education, 43,* 1-7.

[6] In research, a "confederate" is someone who is posing as a participant in research but in reality is working for the researcher. In this study, the confederate was posing as just another student, when in fact, he or she was working for the researcher.

confederate who refuses to enter the car. Students' decisions whether to enter the car and their concern about the driver's drinking were assessed. Results revealed that participants consistently chose to enter the car in all conditions except when the confederate refused. Condition had no effect on participants' reported concern.

___ 2. Does the abstract highlight the research methodology?

Comment: Given the shortness of an abstract, researchers usually can provide only limited details on their methodology. However, even a brief highlight can be helpful to readers who are searching for research reports of interest. Consider Example 3.2.1, which is taken from an abstract. The fact that 1,119 physicians were mailed questionnaires sets it apart from other studies such as those in which small groups of physicians were interviewed.

Example 3.2.1[7]
Excerpt from an abstract that mentions methodology:

Questionnaires were mailed to 1,119 physicians in South Carolina....

Likewise, the information in Example 3.2.2 provides important information about the researchers' methodology since longitudinal studies (studies of participants over an extended period of time) are relatively rare. Even rarer is the use of students as coresearchers in academic research. These features of the methodology are certainly worth mentioning in an abstract because they clearly distinguish this research article from others on the same general topic.

Example 3.2.2[8]
Excerpt from an abstract that mentions methodology:

The research was part of a six-year longitudinal study of student motivation in which students participated as coresearchers.

___ 3. Has the researcher omitted the titles of measures (except when these are the focus of the research)?

Comment: Including the full, formal titles of published measures such as tests,

---

[7] Dickinson, G. E. et al. (1998). Attitudes toward assisted suicide and euthanasia among physicians in South Carolina and Washington. *Omega: Journal of Death and Dying, 36*, 201–218.
[8] Oldfather, P. & Thomas, S. (1998). What does it mean when high school teachers participate in collaborative research with students on literacy motivations? *Teachers College Record, 99*, 647–691.

questionnaires, and scales in an abstract is *usually* inappropriate (see the exception below) because their names take up space that could be used for more important matters. Example 3.3.1 illustrates this problem. It is patterned on a portion of an abstract that recently appeared in a leading journal. Example 3.3.2 illustrates how this flaw could have been avoided.

Example 3.3.1
The portion of an abstract dealing with measurement:

A sample of 483 college males completed the Attitudes Toward Alcohol (Fourth Edition, Revised), the Alcohol Use Questionnaire, and the Manns-Herschfield Quantitative Inventory of Alcohol Dependence (Brief Form).

Example 3.3.2
An improved version of Example 3.3.1:

A sample of 483 college males completed measures of their attitudes toward alcohol, their alcohol use, and their dependence on alcohol.

The exception: If the primary purpose of the research is to evaluate the reliability and validity of one or more specific measures, it would be appropriate to name them in the abstract as well as in the title. This will help readers who are interested in learning about the characteristics of specific measures locate relevant research reports.

____ 4. Are the highlights of the results described?

Comment: The last two sentences in Example 3.4.1 describe the highlights of the results of a study, which is appropriate in an abstract. Notice that the researchers state that incompatibility and lack of emotional support were the *most frequently* cited determinants of divorce. However, they do *not* state how frequently these determinants were cited and what other determinants were cited by the women in the study. In other words, they are reporting only highlights.

Example 3.4.1[9]
A complete abstract with highlights of results reported:

Previous research suggests women's reported causes of divorce vary depending on their SES.[10] However, SES has been routinely defined by husbands' income rather than by the women's personal SES. Further, the

---

[9] Dolan, M. A. & Hoffman, C. D. (1998). Determinants of divorce among women: A reexamination of critical influences. *Journal of Divorce and Remarriage, 28,* 97-106.
[10] SES stands for socioeconomic status.

importance of spousal career support as a determinant of divorce for women has been examined only for highly educated professional women. Utilizing a questionnaire designed for this study, 130 divorced women provided retrospective accounts of factors that led to their divorce. Regardless of women's SES, incompatibility and lack of emotional support were the most frequently cited determinants of divorce. Women divorced fewer than 10 years rated lack of career support as a more important factor in their divorce than did women who had been divorced for a longer time.

Note that there is nothing inherently wrong with giving specific results (and statistics) if space permits and if they are not misleading out of the context of the full research report. Example 3.4.2 illustrates this. Notice, however, that the author still is citing only highlights, for example, by naming only the two most frequently cited reasons for using condoms.

Example 3.4.2[11]

Part of an abstract with some specific results reported as highlights:

Examined the sexual behaviors and safer sex practices of 1,919 college students (aged 18-57 years) attending a commuter university. Survey responses indicate that slightly more than 10% used condoms consistently. The most frequently cited reasons for not using condoms were monogamy (83%) and preferring other forms of birth control (31%). The leading reason for consistent condom use was....

___ 5. Has the researcher avoided making vague references to implications and future research directions?

Comment: Most researchers discuss the implications of their research and directions for future research near the end of their research reports. However, the limited amount of space allotted to abstracts should not be used to make vague references to these matters. Example 3.5.1 is the closing sentence from an abstract. It contains vague references to implications and future research.

Example 3.5.1

Last sentence of an abstract with vague references to implications and future research:

This article concludes with a discussion of both the implications of the results and directions for future research.

---

[11] Prince, A. & Bernard, A. L. (1998). Sexual behaviors and safer sex practices of college students on a commuter campus. *Journal of American College Health, 47,* 11-21.

Example 3.5.1 could safely be omitted from the abstract without causing a loss of important information because most readers will correctly assume that most research reports discuss these elements. An alternative to omitting it is to state something specific about these matters, as illustrated in Example 3.5.2. Notice that in this example, the researcher does not describe the implications but tells us something specific: The implications will be of special interest to a particular group of professionals—school counselors. This will alert school counselors that this research report (among the many hundreds of others on drug abuse) might be of special interest to them. If space does not permit such a long closing sentence, it could be shortened to "Implications for school counselors are discussed."[12]

Example 3.5.2

Improved version of Example 3.5.1 (last sentence of an abstract):

While these results have implications for all professionals who work with adolescents who abuse drugs, special attention is given to the implications for school counselors.

In short, implications and future research do not necessarily need to be mentioned in abstracts. If they are mentioned, however, something specific should be said about them.

___ **6. Overall, is the abstract effective and appropriate?**

Comment: Rate this evaluation question after considering your answers to the earlier ones in this chapter and any additional considerations and concerns you may have. Be prepared to rewrite the abstracts of research reports to which you assign low ratings.

Exercise for Chapter 3

Directions: Evaluate each of the following abstracts (to the extent that it is possible to do so without reading the associated articles) by answering evaluation question number 6 (Overall, is the abstract effective and appropriate?) using a

---

[12] Note that this statement would not be needed if it appeared in an abstract in a journal with a title such as *Research in School Counseling*, since it would be reasonable to expect that all research reports in such a journal would contain discussions of implications for school counselors. Hence, it is not necessary to refer to implications in an abstract unless the researcher can say something about the implications that adds information.

scale from 1 (poor) to 5 (excellent). In the explanations for your ratings, refer to the other five evaluation questions in this chapter.

References for the following abstracts are given in the footnotes. The journals in which they appeared are widely available in large academic libraries, making it possible for you to consult the complete articles if they are assigned by your instructor. More definitive application of the evaluation criteria for abstracts is possible by first reading complete articles and then evaluating their abstracts.

1. *Title:* Femininity, Bulimia, and Distress in College Women[13]

   Abstract: Investigated differences in scores on perceived Distress and Bulimia among 186 college women with varying scores on the Behavioral Self-report of Femininity. Distress was assessed using the Psychological Distress Inventory, and Bulimia was measured using the Bulimia Cognitive Distortions Scale. Ss[14] reporting low numbers of stereotypic feminine behaviors scored lower on the Bulimia Cognitive Distortions Scale than Ss reporting moderate to high numbers of stereotypic feminine behaviors. One factor of the Behavioral Self-report of Femininity, Social Connectedness, made a significant contribution to the prediction of Bulimia scores.

   ### Overall, is the abstract effective and appropriate?
   5   4   3   2   1

Explain your rating:

2. *Title:* Educational Status of Children Who Are Receiving Services in an Urban Family Preservation and Reunification Setting[15]

   Abstract: Examines the educational performance of children who are receiving services from an urban child care service agency, with an emphasis on family preservation and reunification. Participants for the study were 56 children (30 boys and 26 girls), ranging from 1st to 8th grade or between ages 6 and 15. Information on the educational performance of the participants was collected using the Educational Status Form, a 14-item questionnaire. Data included educational performance, attendance pattern, and family status. The majority of the study participants were performing poorly in core academic areas. In addition, the students averaged 16 days absent and almost 9 days tardy. 25% of the participants had already repeated one or more grades. No relationships were reported between school performance and family status. The results of the study, limitations, future research needs, and the need for early intervention are discussed.

   ### Overall, is the abstract effective and appropriate?
   5   4   3   2   1

Explain your rating:

---

[13] Brazelton, E. W., Greene, K. S., Gynther, M., & O'Mell, J. (1998). *Psychological Reports, 83*, 355–363.
[14] *Ss* is a standard abbreviation for *subjects*.
[15] Epstein, M. H., Jayanthi, M., Dennis, K., Dennis, K. L., Hardy, R., Fueyo, V., Frankenberry, E., & McKelvey, J. (1998). *Journal of Emotional and Behavioral Disorders, 6*, 162–169.

3. *Title:* Children's Perspectives on Their Education[16]

Abstract: Sociologists of education were among the first to deal with pupils' perspectives as regards their school life. However, children's points of view on their global educational experience are still rarely explored by sociologists. Although the sociology of childhood is growing fast, it more often covers what adults do to children rather than what children do with what adults do to them. This article discusses some methodological issues involved in the study of children and presents a conceptual framework for approaching the children's points of view on their own education. Based on in-depth interviews of 67 11- to 12-year-old children from Geneva, it deals more particularly with their experience of parental and teacher educational practices and organization. It presents the types of experience these children have of their school and family education and socialization, based on the subtle analyses they make of their parents' and teachers' roles and authority, the emotions they experience vis-a-vis their parents' and teachers' educational practices, and the strategies they develop to face their parents' and teachers' actual or anticipated demands.

Overall, is the abstract effective and appropriate?

5   4   3   2   1

Explain your rating:

4. *Title:* Eating Disorder Symptomatology and Substance Use in College Females[17]

Abstract: The purpose of this study was to examine the relationship between eating disorder symptomatology and substance use (i.e., marijuana, nicotine, cocaine, amphetamines, diet pills, tranquilizers, psychedelics) in a female college student population. A sample of 195 female college students (aged 17-25 yrs) completed the Eating Disorder Inventory, the Quantitative Inventory of Alcohol Disorders, and the Demographic and Drug Use Questionnaire. An insignificant relationship between substance use and eating disorder symptomatology was found. Despite this lack of relationship, relatively high levels of eating disorder symptomatology and problematic alcohol use were found. Implications for college professionals are discussed.

Overall, is the abstract effective and appropriate?

5   4   3   2   1

Explain your rating:

5. *Title:* Reliability of Performance on the Test of Memory and Learning (TOMAL) by an Adolescent Learning Disability Sample[18]

Abstract: The Test of Memory and Learning (TOMAL) is a recent comprehensive memory battery offered to neuropsychologists and standardized on a national sample of children ages 5 years through 19 years. The TOMAL Manual reports very high coefficient alpha internal consistency reliability coefficients for the standardization sample of "normal" children. In the current study, 99 adolescents (aged 12-18 yrs) diagnosed with various learning disabilities in the public schools were administered the TOMAL, and Cronbach's alpha was calculated based on the responses of these 99 adolescents. A matched sample was drawn from the

---

[16] Montandon, C. & Osiek, F. (1998). *Childhood: A Global Journal of Child Research, 5,* 247–263.

[17] Kashubeck, S. & Mintz, L. B. (1996). *Journal of College Student Development, 37,* 396–404.

[18] Reynolds, C. R. (1998). *Educational and Psychological Measurement, 58,* 832–835.

standardization sample and alpha computed for this group. Alpha values in the two groups were highly similar across all 14 subtests. Although adolescents with learning disabilities often have memory deficits, their performance on the TOMAL tends to be as reliable as that of adolescents without learning disabilities.

Overall, is the abstract effective and appropriate?

5 4 3 2 1

Explain your rating:

Notes:

Chapter 4

Evaluating Introductions and Literature Reviews

Research reports in academic journals almost always begin with an introduction in which literature is cited.[1] This integrated introduction and literature review has these five purposes: (a) introduce the problem area, (b) establish its importance, (c) provide an overview of the relevant literature, (d) show how the current study will advance knowledge in the area, and (e) describe the researcher's specific research questions, purposes, or hypotheses, which are usually stated in the last paragraph of the introduction.

This chapter presents evaluation questions regarding the introduction. In the next chapter, the selection and presentation of the literature will be examined more closely.

___ 1. Does the researcher begin by identifying a specific problem area?

Comment: Some researchers start their introductions with statements that are so broad that they fail to identify the specific area for investigation. As the beginning of an introduction to a study on smoking, Example 4.1.1 is deficient. Notice that it fails to identify the specific area of public health that is explored in the research.

Example 4.1.1
Beginning of an introduction that is too broad:

State and local governments expend considerable resources for research on public health issues. The findings of this research are used to formulate public policies that regulate health-related activities within the broader society. In addition to helping establish regulations, public health agencies attempt to educate the public so that individuals have appropriate information when making individual lifestyle decisions that may affect their health.

---

[1] In theses and dissertations, the first chapter is usually an introduction, with relatively few references to the literature. This is followed by a second chapter that provides a comprehensive literature review.

Example 4.1.2. illustrates a more appropriate beginning for a research report on a public health issue—in this case, the demographics (i.e., background characteristics such as age and education) of smokers and nonsmokers.

Example 4.1.2[2]

An improved version of Example 4.1.1:

Cigarette smoking is the single largest cause of premature and avoidable death and disability in the United States (U.S Surgeon General, 1989). Although rates of adult smoking have been declining since the publication of the 1964 Surgeon General's Report, epidemiological data suggest that these successes have not uniformly been distributed among the population. Rather….

Making a decision as to whether a researcher has started the introduction by being reasonably specific often involves some subjectivity. As a general rule, the researcher should get to the point rather quickly without using valuable journal space to outline a broad problem area that he or she has not directly studied.

___ 2. Does the researcher establish the importance of the problem area?

Comment: Researchers select research problems they believe are important, and they should specifically address this belief early in their introductions. Often this is done by citing previously published statistics that indicate how widespread a problem is, how many people are affected by it, and so on. Example 4.2.1 illustrates how one researcher did this in a study on the relationship between homework and achievement. Note that it might be safe to assume that readers of a journal on educational psychology (in which this appeared) already know that homework is an important issue. However, many might not know how many students do homework or how much time they spend on it. Other things being equal, readers will have more confidence in researchers who provide such specific evidence on the persuasiveness and, thus, importance of the topic they are investigating.

---

[2] Rose, J. S., Chassin, L., Presson, C. C., & Sherman, S. J. (1996). Demographic factors in adult smoking status: Mediating and moderating influences. *Psychology of Addictive Behaviors, 10*, 28-37.

Example 4.2.1[3]

Beginning an introduction that includes statistics to establish the importance of a problem area:

Homework, defined as tasks assigned to students by school teachers that are meant to be performed during nonschool hours (Cooper, 1989, p. 7), is a pervasive teaching strategy. The National Assessment of Educational Progress found that two-thirds of students in 4th, 8th, and 11th grades reported doing homework and the percentage was increasing over time (Anderson et al., 1986). Among 8th graders, the average amount of time spent on homework is about 1 hour each day (Walberg, 1991).

Note that the statistics a researcher cites in order to establish the importance of his or her problem should be closely aligned with the specific problem that was investigated. For example, there is a very large body of academic literature on homosexuality.[4] It would be superfluous to have each research report on this topic start with statistics on the percentage of the population that is self-identified as homosexual. Instead, if a researcher is introducing a study on adolescent suicide among gay adolescents, for example, he or she might cite statistics on suicide rates among this specific population.

Instead of providing statistics on the prevalence of problems, researchers sometimes use other strategies to convince readers of their problems' importance. One approach is to show that a topic is of current interest because of corporate or government actions such as the passage of the Americans with Disabilities Act. Another is to show that prominent people or influential authors have considered and addressed the issue that is being researched. Example 4.2.2 illustrates the latter technique, which was used to help establish the importance of a study on whether inducing empathy for a member of a stigmatized group improves attitudes toward that group.

Example 4.2.2[5]

Excerpt from the beginning of an introduction that uses a nonstatistical argument to establish the importance of a problem:

What is the social significance of books such as *Manchild in the Promised Land* (Brown, 1965), *House Made of Dawn* (Momaday, 1968), *One Flew Over the Cuckoo's Nest* (Kesey, 1962), *The Color Purple* (Walker, 1982)…and *Longtime Companion* (Wlodkowski & Rene, 1990)?

---

[3] Cooper, H., Lindsay, J. J., Nye, B., & Greathouse, S. (1998). Relationships among attitudes about homework, amount of homework assigned and completed, and student achievement. *Journal of Educational Pschology*, *90*, 70-83.

[4] A recent search of the PsycINFO database of psychological literature alone yielded 649 journal articles on this topic.

[5] Batson, C. D. et al. (1997). Empathy and attitudes: Can feeling for a member of a stigmatized group improve feelings toward the group? *Journal of Personality and Social Psychology*, *72*, 105-118.

We believe that each of these works, and many similar ones, seek to improve attitudes toward a stigmatized group—a racial or cultural minority, people with some social stigma, disability, or disease.

The strategy used is to induce the audience to feel empathy for one or a few members of the stigmatized group....

Finally, a researcher may attempt to establish the nature and importance of a problem by citing anecdotal evidence or personal experience. While this is arguably the weakest way to establish the importance of a problem, a unique and interesting anecdote might convince readers that the problem is important enough to investigate.

A caveat: When you apply evaluation question 2 to the introduction of a research report, do *not* confuse the importance of a problem with your personal interest in the problem. It is possible to have little personal interest in a problem yet still recognize that a researcher has established its importance. On the other hand, it is possible to have a strong personal interest in a problem but judge that the researcher has failed to make a strong argument (or has failed to present convincing evidence) to establish its importance.

___ 3. Is the introduction an essay that logically moves from topic to topic?

Comment: Introductions that typically fail on this evaluation question are organized around references rather than topics. For example, a researcher might first summarize Smith's study, then summarize Jones' study, and so on. The result is a series of annotations that are strung together. This fails to guide readers through the literature, showing how the references relate to each other and what they mean as a whole.

In contrast, a topical introduction is organized around topics and subtopics with references cited as needed, often in groups of two or more articles. For example, if four research reports support a certain point, the point usually should be stated with all four references cited together. This is illustrated in Example 4.3.1. Notice that there is one reference for the point made in the first sentence while there are four references cited for the point made in the second sentence.

Example 4.3.1[6]

An excerpt from a literature review with references cited in groups:

Based on these findings, state and federal governments have tried to reduce street violent crimes through aggressive law enforcement against drug sellers and users (Popkin, Olson, Lurigio, Gwiasda, and Carter, 1995). In high-crime areas such as public housing projects, aggressive policing and tenant empowerment programs have been temporarily effective in reducing drug selling and drug-related violent and property crimes and in fostering a sense of safety and community improvement among residents (National Institute of Justice 1995b, 1996; Popkin et al. 1995; Sherman, Shaw, and Rogan, 1995).

Of course, when a researcher is discussing a reference that is crucial to a point he or she is making, that reference should be discussed in more detail than was done in Example 4.3.1. However, because research reports in academic journals arc expected to be relatively brief, this should be done sparingly and only for the most important related literature.

___ 4. Has the researcher provided conceptual definitions of key terms?

Comment: Often, researchers will pause at appropriate points in their introductions to offer formal conceptual definitions[7] such as the one shown in Example 4.4.1. Note that it is acceptable for a researcher to cite a previously published definition.

Example 4.4.1[8]

A conceptual definition provided in an introduction:

Emotional intelligence has been defined as "the *ability* [italics added] to monitor one's own and others' emotions, to discriminate among them, and to use the information to guide one's thinking and actions" (Salovey & Mayer, 1990, p. 189). A number of researchers thus view the capacity to process affective information as a "mental ability" or "aptitude" in the conventional sense.

---

[6] Montalvo-Barbot, A. (1997). Crime in Puerto Rico: Drug trafficking, money laundering, and the poor. *Crime and Delinquency, 43,* 533-547.
[7] A *conceptual* definition seeks to identify a term using only general concepts but with enough specificity that the term is not confused with other related terms or concepts. As such, they resemble dictionary definitions. In contrast, an *operational definition* describes the physical process used to examine something.
[8] Davies, M., Stankov, L., & Roberts, R. D. (1998). Emotional intelligence: In search of an elusive construct. *Journal of Personality and Social Psychology, 75,* 989-1015.

Sometimes important terms are not formally defined, but their meanings are made clear by the context of the introduction. For instance, researchers sometimes cite examples of what is and is not covered by a key term they are using, which helps to define it.

At times, researchers may not offer either formal definitions or in-context definitions, and you may judge that the terms have such widespread commonly held definitions that they do not need to be defined. For example, in a report of research on various methods of teaching handwriting, a researcher may not offer a definition of handwriting in his or her introduction, and you might judge this to be acceptable. Of course, you will expect the researcher to describe later how handwriting was measured (i.e., the *operational definition*) when you get to the details of the methods used to conduct the research.

In sum, this evaluation question should not be applied mechanically by looking to see if there is a specific statement of a definition. The mere absence of one does not necessarily mean that a researcher has failed on this evaluation question. Instead, you may judge that a definition is simply not needed.

___ 5. Has the researcher indicated the basis for "factual" statements?

Comment: Sometimes researchers make statements that sound like "facts" without referring to their source. As you know from freshman composition, this is highly undesirable. A common statement of this type is the unsubstantiated claim that interest in a problem is growing or that the number of people affected by a problem is increasing, which is illustrated in Example 4.5.1. Notice that not only is the "fact" not substantiated with a reference to its source, it is also vague because "dramatically" is not defined. Example 4.5.2 is an improved version.

Example 4.5.1
An unreferenced "factual" claim:

Interest in child abuse and mistreatment has increased dramatically in recent years.

Example 4.5.2[9]
Improved version of Example 4.5.1:

Child maltreatment incident reports increased by 50% between 1988 and 1993, totaling more than 2.9 million reports in 1993 (McCurdy & Daro, 1994). Much of this increase can be attributed to....

---

[9] Akin, B. A. & Gregoire, T. K. (1997). Parents' views on child welfare's response to addiction. *Families in Society: The Journal of Contemporary Human Services, 78*, 393-404.

Note, however, it is appropriate for researchers to express their opinions in introductions as long as the context makes it clear that they are opinions and not "facts." In Example 4.5.3, the researchers express what is clearly an opinion because of the use of the word "contend."

Example 4.5.3[10]

A statement properly identified as an opinion:

We contend that preservice teacher education does not include sufficient attention to gender equity.

___ 6. Do the specific research purposes, questions, or hypotheses logically flow from the introductory material?

Comment: Typically, the specific research purposes, questions, or hypotheses that drive a research study are stated in the last paragraph of the introduction.[11] The material preceding them should set the stage and logically lead to them. For example, if a researcher argues that research methods used by previous researchers are not well suited for answering certain research questions, you would not be surprised to learn that his or her research purpose is to reexamine the research questions using alternative research methods. Likewise, if a researcher points out in the introduction that there are certain specific gaps in what is known about a problem area (that is, the previously published literature has not covered certain subtopics), you would not be surprised to learn that the purpose of the study that is being introduced is designed to fill those gaps. Example 4.6.1 is the last paragraph in the introduction to a research report. In it, the researchers summarize the literature that they just reviewed, pointing to certain specific gaps in the literature. This sets the stage for the specific research purpose, which is stated in the last sentence of the example.

Example 4.6.1[12]

Last paragraph of an introduction (beginning with a summary of the research that was reviewed and ending with a statement of the research purpose in the last sentence):

Most studies that have considered psychological variables related to exercise have focused on maintenance of exercise by volunteers in

---

[10] Campbell, P. B. & Sanders, J. (1997). Uninformed but interested: Findings of a national survey on gender equity in preservice education. *Journal of Teacher Education, 48,* 69-75.

[11] Some researchers state their research purposes, questions, or hypotheses in general terms near the beginning of their introductions and then restate them more specifically near the end.

[12] Wilcox, S. & Storandt, M. (1996). Relations among age, exercise, and psychological variables in a community sample of women. *Health Psychology, 15,* 110-113.

structured exercise programs. They tell us little about sedentary individuals who have no interest in initiating exercise. It is important to understand the self-efficacy, attitudes, and self-motivation of these sedentary individuals if we are to design interventions that will induce them to exercise. Furthermore, many of the studies of the psychological correlates of exercise behavior in older adults have focused on men, often in cardiac rehabilitation programs. Overall, very little is known about how women in unstructured exercise programs think about exercise. Thus, in this study we examined exercise self-efficacy, attitudes about exercise, and self-motivation for exercise in a community sample of exercising and nonexercising adult women between the ages of 20 and 85.

___ **7. Overall, is the introduction effective and appropriate?**

Comment: Rate this evaluation question after considering your answers to the earlier ones in this chapter and any additional considerations and concerns you may have. Be prepared to explain your overall evaluation.

Exercise for Chapter 4

Directions: Read several research reports in academic journals on a topic of interest to you. Apply the evaluation questions in this chapter to the introductions, and select the one to which you have given the highest ratings. Bring it to class for discussion. Be prepared to discuss its strengths and weaknesses.

Chapter 5

A Closer Look at Evaluating Literature Reviews

As you learned in the previous chapter, literature reviews are usually integrated into the researchers' introductory statements. In that chapter, the emphasis was on the functions of the introduction and the most salient and easy-to-evaluate characteristics of the literature review. In this chapter, we will examine evaluation questions regarding the presentation of the literature that are important but often difficult to evaluate.

___ 1. If there is extensive literature on a topic, has the researcher been selective?

Comment: Of course, you may not know if the research on a topic is extensive unless you have studied the topic in detail or unless the researcher makes a statement as to its breadth. Even in the absence of this information, you can still spot certain flaws related to this evaluation question. First, look for long strings of references used to support a single point or position. This is often a sign that the researcher has not been selective in choosing research to cite.[1] Example 5.1.1 illustrates this flaw. Example 5.1.2 shows an improved version. Notice that "e.g." (meaning "for example") is appropriately used in Example 5.1.2.

Example 5.1.1[2]
Unselective referencing (inappropriate):

Exactly how attitudes influence behavior is one of the chief questions facing contemporary social psychology (Appleton, 1993; Barnes, 1993; Chadoff, 1992; Davidson, 1999; Freedman, 2000; Fry, 1999; Galt, 1997; Greeverson, 1996; Hadley & Smith, 1995; Hoover & Johnson, 1998; James, 2000; Kelp, 2001; Koontz, Doe, & Jones, 1999; Kibler & Loone, 1999; [and so on]).

---

[1] Long strings of references for a single point are more justifiable in a thesis or dissertation, especially if the committee that is evaluating it expects a student to produce a comprehensive review to demonstrate that he or she can locate all the literature related to a topic.

[2] This example is based on one that appears in Harlow, H. F. (1962). Fundamental principles for preparing psychology journal articles. *Journal of Comparative and Physiological Psychology, 55,* 893-896.

Example 5.1.2[3]

Selective referencing (citing only important references):

Exactly how attitudes influence behavior is one of the chief questions facing contemporary social psychology and has been explored in hundreds of studies (e.g., Eagly & Chaiken, 1993; Terry & Hogg, in press). Probably the best known attempt at answering this question has been made by the theory of reasoned action (Fishbein & Ajzen, 1975) and its recent extension, the theory of planned behavior (Ajzen, 1991). These theories....

___ 2. Is the literature review critical?

Comment: When reviewing previously published studies, a researcher should consider their strengths and weaknesses. Articles that are reasonably strong may be cited without comment on their methodological merits. Also, a researcher may feel it unnecessary to point out weaknesses in previously published research reports when their results have been corroborated (or replicated) by other research that is also cited in the review. However, when the results of several studies contradict one another, researchers should usually point out which ones may be more dependable than the others or note that all are weak when that is the case. Example 5.2.1, which is taken from the introduction to a study on clinical interviews of bilingual Hispanics, illustrates the technique.

Example 5.2.1[4]

Critical excerpt from a literature review:

A general problem with the interview language studies is that they were based on extremely small samples. Del Castillo's (1970) observations were based on a few interviews, Marcos (1976) inteviewed only 10 patients, and Price and Cuellar (1981) interviewed only 32 patients. Thus, the discrepant outcomes may reflect the unreliability produced by small sample size in each study.

Sometimes criticism is subtle, as in Example 5.2.2 where the researchers have hedged their generalizations from the literature as indicated by the italicized words. Notice how these words suggest that caution should be used

---

[3] This example is a modification of a statement made by Wellen, J. M., Hogg, M. A., & Terry, D. J. (1998). Group norms and attitude-behavior consistency: The role of group salience and mood. *Group Dynamics, Theory, Research, and Practice, 2,* 48-56.
[4] Malgady, R. G. (1998). Symptom severity in bilingual Hispanics as a function of clinician ethnicity and language of interview. *Psychological Assessment, 10,* 120-127.

when considering the results. If you read the example a second time, leaving out the italicized words, you will get a very different impression of the state of knowledge on this topic.

Example 5.2.2[5]

Excerpt from a literature review (subtle criticism expressing caution, italics added):

However, though less attention has been given to personality factors, there is *some* evidence that affective-based or dispositional correlates are related to emotional exhaustion (Cordes & Dougherty, 1993). Consequently, *it might be that* affective personality dispositions are accounting for the relationship between emotional exhaustion and various work outcomes. Lee and Ashforth (1996) noted the need for research *providing additional clarification* of these *proposed* relationships.

Of course, a researcher might also want to point out strengths of particular studies along the way—especially if they are promising studies on which the current one is closely based.

___ 3. Is current research cited?

Comment: You can check the currency of the literature by noting whether research published in recent years has been cited. Keep in mind, however, that relevance to the research topic is more important than currency. A ten-year-old study that is highly relevant may deserve more attention than a less relevant one that was recently published. Also note that researchers may wish to show the historical links of a line of research, which helps establish its legitimacy. In Example 5.3.1, the researcher links a particular finding back to Piaget, an important and widely-cited researcher in child development. This historical linkage adds support to the point being made by suggesting that it has stood the test of time by being replicated more recently.

Example 5.3.1[6]

An excerpt from a literature review showing historical links:

According to research carried out by Piaget (1932) and subsequently by Wimmer, Gruber, and Perner (1984) and Strichartz and Burton (1990), young children have little of no understanding of lying as deceptive

---

[5] Wright, T. A. & Cropanzano, R. (1998). Emotional exhaustion as a predictor of job performance and voluntary turnover. *Journal of Applied Psychology, 83*, 486-493.
[6] Siegal, M. (1998). Preschoolers' understanding of lies and innocent and negligent mistakes. *Developmental Psychology, 2*, 332–341.

statements intended to mislead others. They regard all falsehoods as lies and do not recognize that a genuine mistake by a speaker who believes that he or she has made a true statement is not a lie.

___ 4. Has the researcher distinguished between research, theory, and opinion?

Comment: Researchers should use wording that helps readers understand whether the cited literature presents research results, theory, or opinions.

For indicating that a citation is research-based, there are a variety of options, some of which are shown in Example 5.4.1.

Example 5.4.1
Examples of key terms and expressions indicating that a citation is research based:

Recent data suggest that….

In laboratory experiments….

Recent test scores suggest….

Group A has outperformed its counterparts on measures of….

Research on XYZ has ….

Data from surveys comparing….

Doe (1999) found that the rate….

These studies have greatly increased our knowledge of….

In addition, if a researcher cites a specific statistic from the literature [e.g., African Americans have one of the highest rates of smoking (29%)….[7]], it is safe to assume that research is being cited.

When citing a premise from theory, a researcher should simply use the word "theory" and distinguish it from research findings related to the theory, which is illustrated in Example 5.4.2.

Example 5.4.2[8]
Excerpt indicating the distinction between theory and research (italics added):

---

[7] Robinson, L. A. & Klesges, R. C. (1997). Ethnic and group differences in risk factors for smoking onset. *Health Psychology, 16,* 499-505.
[8] Ibid.

premature transition to adult activity. Thus,…. In a *number of studies* rebellious children have been found to be significantly more likely to smoke (Chassin, …1986). *Research* has also….

Sometimes researchers cite the opinions of others. When they do this, they should word their statements in such a way that the reader is made aware that opinions are being cited. Example 5.4.3 shows some examples of key words and phrases that researchers sometimes use to do this.

Example 5.4.3
Examples of key terms and expressions indicating that an opinion is being cited:

Jones (1999) has argued that….

These kinds of assumptions were….

Despite this speculation….

These arguments predict….

This logical suggestion….

___ **5. Overall, is the literature review portion of the introduction appropriate?**

Comment: Rate this evaluation question after considering your answers to the earlier ones in this chapter and any additional considerations and concerns you may have. Be prepared to explain your overall evaluation.

Exercise for Chapter 5

Directions: Read several research reports in academic journals on a topic of interest to you. Apply the evaluation questions in this chapter to the literature reviews in their introductions, and select the one to which you gave the highest ratings. Bring it to class for discussion. Be prepared to discuss its strengths and weaknesses.

Notes:

Chapter 6

Evaluating Samples When Researchers Generalize

Immediately after the introduction, which includes a literature review, most researchers insert a main heading called "Method." In the method section, they almost universally begin by describing the people they studied—their sample. This description is usually prefaced with one of these subheadings: "Participants,"[1] or "Subjects."

A *population* is any group in which a researcher is ultimately interested. It may be large such as all registered voters in Pennsylvania, or it may be small such as all members of a local teachers' association. Researchers often study only a *sample* (i.e., a subset of a population) for the sake of efficiency and then *generalize* their results to the population, that is, they infer that the data they collected by studying the sample are similar to the data they would have obtained by studying the entire population.

Because many researchers do not explicitly state whether they are attempting to generalize, you will often need to make a judgment on this matter in order to decide whether to apply the evaluation questions in this chapter to a research report you are evaluating. Does the researcher *imply* that the results apply to some larger population? Does the researcher discuss the implications of his or her research for a larger group than the one directly studied? Note that the answers to these questions may be found anywhere in a research report, so you will need to read the entire report before answering them. If the answers are clearly "yes," you should apply the evaluation questions in this chapter to the article you have read. Note that in Chapter 7 the evaluation of samples when researchers are *not* generalizing is considered.

___ 1. Was random sampling used?

Comment: Using random sampling (like drawing names out of a hat) yields an *unbiased* sample (i.e., a sample that does not systematically favor any particular type of individual or group in the selection process). If a sample is unbiased and

---

[1] For most of the 1900s, the standard subheading was "Subjects." Near the end of the century, "Participants" became popular. The latter term conveys the idea that the people being studied have consented to participate after being informed of the nature of the research project.

large, researchers are likely to make sound generalizations. (Sample size will be discussed later in this chapter.)

The desirability of using random samples as the basis for making generalizations is so widely recognized among professional researchers that they are almost certain to mention its use if, in fact, they have used it. This is illustrated in Example 6.1.1. If all 1,000 of the selected principals agree to participate in the research study, the researchers will be able to generalize with considerable confidence to all principals who belong to the National Organization of Secondary Principals.

Example 6.1.1[2]

From the membership list of the National Association of Secondary Principals (NASP), the national organization created a random sample of 1,000 principals [to be contacted in this study].

___ 2. If random sampling was used, was it stratified?

Comment: Researchers use *stratified random sampling* by drawing individuals separately at random from different strata (i. e., subgroups) within a population. Suppose a researcher wanted to survey licensed clinical psychologists in a large city. To stratify, he or she might divide the population into four subgroups: those who practice on the north side of town, those who practice on the east side, and so on. Then he or she could draw a fixed percentage at random from each side of town. The result will be a sample that is geographically representative. For instance, if 40% of the population practices on the west side, then 40% of the sample will be from the west side.

Stratifying will improve a sample only if the stratification variable (geography in our example) is related to the variables to be studied. For instance, if the researcher is planning to study how psychologists work with illicit substance abusers, stratifying on geography will improve the sample if the various areas of the city tend to have different types of drug problems, which may require different treatment modalities.

Note that *geography* is often an excellent variable on which to stratify because people tend to cluster geographically based on many variables that are important in the social and behavioral sciences. For example, they often cluster according to race/ethnicity, income/personal wealth, language preference, religion, and so on. Thus, a geographically representative sample is likely to be representative in terms of these other variables as well.

---

[2] Price, J. H. & Everett, S. A. (1997). A national assessment of secondary school principals' perceptions of violence in schools. *Health Education & Behavior, 24,* 218-229.

Sometimes researchers want to stratify but are unable to do so, as illustrated in Example 6.2.1, which is a continuation of Example 6.1.1. Note that the researchers acknowledged the desirability of stratifying in their study of violence in the schools, recognizing that there may be different patterns and incidence rates of violence in different types of geographical areas.

Example 6.2.1[3]

A stratification sampling strategy based on a nationally representative sample of secondary schools by location of school was not possible because the proportion of secondary schools in urban, suburban, and rural communities could not be determined (personal communication, National Center for Educational Statistics, 1994).

Note that if random sampling without stratification is used, the technique is called *simple random sampling*. If stratification is used, it is called *stratified random sampling*.

Despite the almost universal acceptance that an unbiased sample obtained through simple or stratified random sampling is highly desirable for making generalizations, the vast majority of research from which researchers wish to make generalizations is based on studies in which nonrandom (biased) samples were used. There are three major reasons for this:

1. Even though a random selection of names has been drawn, the researcher may not be able to convince all those selected to participate in the research project. For example, even though the researchers who wrote the material in Example 6.1.1 contacted the 1,000 principals three times by mail, only 58% responded. Note that those who responded may be systematically different from those who did not in many important ways (e.g., because they were less interested in the topic or were more professionally active and, thus, have less time to participate in research). Thus, the bias created by the failure of many to participate could seriously affect the results of the study.

2. Many researchers have limited resources—limited time, money, and assistance to conduct research. Often they will reach out for whomever is readily accessible or convenient to use as participants.

3. For some populations, it is difficult to identify all members. If a researcher cannot do this, he or she obviously cannot give each of them an equal chance of having their names drawn. Examples of populations of this type are the homeless in a large city and successful burglars (i.e., those who have never been caught).

Because so many researchers study nonrandom samples, it is unrealistic to count failures on the first two evaluation questions in this chapter as fatal flaws

---

[3] Ibid.

in research methodology. If journal editors routinely refused to publish research reports with this type of deficiency, there would be very little, if any, published research on most of the important problems in the social and behavioral sciences. Thus, when researchers use nonrandom samples when attempting to generalize, the additional evaluation questions raised below should be applied in order to distinguish between studies from which it might be reasonable to make tentative, cautious generalizations and those that are hopelessly flawed in this respect.

___ 3. If the randomness of a sample is impaired by the refusal to participate by some of those selected, is the rate of participation reasonably high?

Comment: Defining "reasonably high" is problematic. For example, a professional survey organization, with trained personnel and substantial resources, would be concerned if it had a response rate of less than 85% when conducting a national survey by phone or in person. On the other hand, researchers with limited resources using mailed questionnaires often are satisfied with a return rate as low as 60%—especially because rates of returns to mailed surveys are often notoriously poor. As a very rough rule-of-thumb, then, response rates of substantially less than 60% raise extremely serious concerns about the generalizability of the findings.

The percentages mentioned in the previous paragraph should not be applied mechanically, however, since you may decide to make exceptions for instances in which participation in the research is burdensome, invasive, or raises sensitive issues—factors that might make it difficult to get a high rate of participation. For instance, if a researcher needed to draw samples of blood from students on campus to estimate the incidence of HIV infection or needed to put a sample of students through a series of physical fitness tests that spanned several days for a study in sports psychology, you might judge a participation rate of substantially less than 60% to be reasonable in light of the particulars of the research, keeping in mind that any generalizations would be highly tenuous.

When applying this evaluation question, you may also wish to consider how much effort a researcher put into trying to obtain a high rate of participation. For example, if a researcher contacted those who were selected several times (by phone, by mail, or in person) and still had a response rate of less than 60%, you might reach the conclusion that this is the highest rate of return that might be expected for the researcher's particular research problem and population. In effect, you might judge that this might be the best that can be done, keeping in mind that generalizations from such a sample are exceedingly risky.

_____ **4. If the randomness of a sample is impaired by the refusal to participate by some of those selected, is there reason to believe that the participants and nonparticipants are similar on relevant variables?**

Comment: Sometimes researchers have information about those who do not participate, which allows for a comparison with those who did. For example, a researcher might note the zip codes in which returned questionnaires were posted. This might allow a researcher to determine whether those in affluent neighborhoods were more responsive than those in less affluent ones.[4]

When participants drop out of studies before their completion (a failure to participate fully), researchers often can compare the pretest data for those who dropped out and those who remained in the study. Example 6.4.1 illustrates this.

Example 6.4.1[5]

In a longitudinal study of parent alcoholism and its effects on adolescents, ten percent of the adolescents were not available or refused to participate at the time of the follow-up (i.e., the nonparticipants). Analysis of the results from the Time 1 (pretest) data revealed that the nonparticipants did not differ significantly from the participants in terms of their age, gender, the severity of their parents' alcoholism, or occupational status.

Knowing that the nonparticipants and the participants are similar on crucial variables increases our confidence that the results may be generalizable to the entire population, which, of course, includes those who would be inclined to participate as well as those who would not be inclined to do so.

_____ **5. If a sample from which a researcher wants to generalize was not selected at random, is it at least drawn from the target group for the generalization?**

Comment: There are many instances in the published literature in which a researcher studied one type of participant (e.g., college freshmen) and used the data to make generalizations to an entirely different target group (e.g., public school students). If a researcher does not have the wherewithal to at least tap into the target group of interest, it might be better if he or she left the research to others with resources and contacts that give them access to members of the target group.

---

[4] If such a bias were detected, statistical adjustments might be made to correct for it.
[5] This example is patterned loosely on material in Chassin, L., Curran, P. J., Hussong, A. M., & Colder, C. R. (1996). *Journal of Abnormal Psychology, 105*, 70-80.

___ 6. If a sample from which a researcher wants to generalize was not selected at random, is it at least reasonably diverse?

Comment: Did a researcher generalize to all college students after studying only students attending a small religious college in which 99% of the students have the same ethnic/racial background? Did a researcher generalize to men and women regarding the relationship between exercise and health after studying only men attending a cardiac unit's exercise program? An answer of "yes" to these types of questions might cause you to give a low rating to this evaluation question.

___ 7. If a sample from which a researcher wants to generalize was not selected at random, does the researcher explicitly discuss this limitation?

Comment: While researchers may discuss the limitations of their methodology (including sampling) any place in their reports, many include a discussion of them in the discussion/conclusions section at the end. Examples 6.7.1 and 6.7.2 illustrate this.

Example 6.7.1[6]
Statement of limitation in sampling:

…the patients examined in this study were a somewhat higher functioning group than typically found in a cross section of outpatients with social phobia. Studies of social success in more representative samples are needed to determine whether these findings apply to all people with social phobia.

Example 6.7.2[7]
Statement of limitation in sampling:

Despite the limitations of having examined only one district within a single state, our findings raise critical questions about the eventual success of the state's reform. Will the teachers be more likely to change.…

Such acknowledgments of limitations do not improve researchers' ability to generalize. However, they do perform two important functions: (a) they

---

[6] Wallace, S. T. & Alden, L. E. (1997). Social phobia and positive social events: The price of success. *Journal of Abnormal Psychology, 106,* 416-424.

[7] Miller, S. D., Hayes, C. T., & Atkinson, T. S. (1997). State efforts to improve students' reading and language arts achievement: Does the left hand know what the right is doing? *Reading Research and Instruction, 36,* 267-286.

serve as warnings to naïve readers regarding the problem of generalizing and (b) they reassure all readers that the researchers are aware of a serious flaw in their methodology, a sign of the researchers' overall competence.

___ 8. Has the author described relevant demographics of the sample?

Comment: A researcher should describe the relevant demographics (i.e., background characteristics). For example, when studying registered nurses' attitudes toward assisted suicide, it would be relevant to know their religious affiliations. For studying consumers' preferences, it would be helpful to know their economic status.

In addition to demographics that are directly relevant to the variables being studied, it is usually desirable to give an overall demographic profile, including variables such as age, gender, race/ethnicity, and highest level of education. This is especially important when a sample of convenience has been used because readers will want to visualize the particular participants who were part of such a sample.

___ 9. Is the overall size of the sample adequate?

Comment: Students who are new to research methods are sometimes surprised to learn that there often is no simple answer to the question of how large a sample should be. First, it depends in part on how much error a researcher is willing to tolerate. For public opinion polls, a sample size of 1,500 drawn at random produces a margin of error of about one to three percentage points. A sample size of 400 produces a margin of error of about four to six percentage points.[8] If a researcher is trying to predict the outcome of a close election, clearly a sample size of 400 would be inadequate.[9]

Responding to a public opinion poll takes little time and may be of interest to many participants. Other types of studies, however, may require extensive cooperation and effort on the part of participants as well as the expenditure of considerable resources on the part of the researchers. Under such circumstances, it may be unrealistic to expect a researcher to use hundreds of participants. Thus, you should ask whether the researchers used a reasonable number given the particular circumstances of their studies. Would it have been an unreasonable burden to use substantially more participants? Is the number of par-

---

[8] The exact size of the margin of error depends on whether the sample was stratified and other sampling issues that are beyond the scope of this book.

[9] With a sample of only 400, there would need to be an eight to ten percentage point *difference* between the two candidates to make a reliable prediction (i.e., statistically significant prediction) based on a sample of this size.

ticipants so low that there is little hope of making sound generalizations? Would you base an important decision on the results of the study given the number of participants that was used? Your subjective answers to these types of questions will guide you on this evaluation question.[10]

It is important to keep in mind that a large sample size does not compensate for a bias in sampling due to the failure to use random sampling, that is, using large numbers of unrepresentative participants does not get around the problem of their unrepresentativeness.

___10. Is there a sufficient number of participants in each subgroup that is reported on separately?

Comment: Consider the hypothetical information in Example 6.10.1, where the numbers of participants in each subgroup are indicated by *n*, and the mean (average) scores are indicated by *m*.

> **Example 6.10.1**
> A random sample of 100 college freshmen were surveyed on their knowledge of alcoholism. Their mean (*m*) scores out of a maximum of 25 were as follows: White ($m = 18.5$, $n = 78$), African American ($m = 20.1$, $n = 11$), Hispanic/Latino(a) ($m = 19.9$, $n = 9$) and Chinese American ($m = 17.9$, $n = 2$).

The numbers of participants in the last three subgroups in the example are so small that it would be inappropriate to generalize from them to their respective populations. The researcher should either obtain larger numbers of them or refrain from reporting on them separately. Notice that there is nothing wrong with indicating ethnic/racial backgrounds such as the fact that there were two Chinese American participants as part of the description of the demographics of the sample. Instead, the problem is that the number of them is too small to justify calculating a mean and making an inference about a population of Chinese Americans.

___11. Has informed consent been obtained?

Comment: It is almost always a good idea to get written, informed consent from the participants in a study. Participants should be informed of the nature of the

---

[10] There are statistical methods for estimating optimum sample sizes under various assumptions. While these methods are beyond the scope of this book, note that they do not take account of the practical matters raised here.

study and, at least in general terms, the nature of their involvement. They should also be informed of their right to withdraw from the study at any time without penalty. Typically, researchers report only very briefly on this matter, as illustrated in Example 6.11.1. It is unrealistic to expect much more detail than shown here. Note that this evaluation question also appears in the next chapter for reasons that you will learn when you read it.

Example 6.11.1
Brief description of informed consent:

Students from the departmental subject pool volunteered to participate in this study for course credit. Prior to participating in the study, students were given an informed consent form that had been approved by the university's institutional review board. The form described the experiment as "a study of social interactions between male and female students." All students who had volunteered gave their written consent.

There will be times when you judge that the study is so innocuous that informed consent might not be needed. A good example is an observational study in which people are observed in public places while the observers are in plain view. Under such circumstances, privacy would not normally be expected.

___ **12. Overall, is the sample appropriate for generalizing?**

Comment: Rate this evaluation question after considering your answers to the earlier ones in this chapter and any additional considerations and concerns you may have. Be prepared to discuss your response to this evaluation question.

Concluding Comment

Although a primary goal of much research in all the sciences is to make sound generalizations from samples to populations, researchers in the social and behavioral sciences face special problems regarding access to and cooperation from samples of humans. Unlike other published lists of criteria for evaluating samples, I have urged you to be pragmatic when making these evaluations. A researcher may have some relatively serious flaws in sampling, yet you may conclude that he or she did a reasonable job under the circumstances he or she faced. However, this does not preclude the need to be exceedingly cautious in making generalizations from studies with weak samples. Our confidence in certain generalizations based on weak samples can be increased, however, if various researchers with different patterns of weaknesses in their sampling methods arrive at similar conclusions when studying the same problems.

Exercise for Chapter 6

Directions: Locate several research reports in academic journals in which the researchers are concerned with generalizing from a sample to a population, and apply the evaluation questions in this chapter. Select the one to which you gave the highest overall rating and bring it to class for discussion. Be prepared to discuss its strengths and weaknesses.

Chapter 7

Evaluating Samples When Researchers Do *Not* Generalize

As you know from the previous chapter, researchers often study samples in order to make inferences about the populations from which the samples were drawn. This process is known as generalizing.

Not all research is aimed at generalizing. Here are the major reasons why:

1. Researchers often conduct *pilot studies*. These are designed to determine the feasibility of methods for studying specific research problems. For example, a novice researcher who wants to conduct an interview study of the social dynamics of safe sex practices among high school students might conduct a pilot study to determine, among other things, how much cooperation can be obtained from school personnel for such a study, what percentage of the parents give permission for their children to participate in interviews on this topic, whether students have difficulty understanding the interview questions and whether they are embarrassed by them, the optimum length of the interviews, and so on. After the research techniques are refined in a pilot study with a sample of convenience, a more definitive study with a more appropriate sample for generalizing might be conducted. Note that it is not uncommon for journals to publish reports of pilot studies, especially if they yield interesting results and point to promising directions for future research. Also note that while many researchers will explicitly identify their pilot studies as such (by using the term "pilot study"), at other times you will need to infer that a study is a pilot study from statements such as "In this preliminary study, the...."

2. Some researchers focus on *developing and testing theories*. A theory is a proposition or set of propositions that provides a cohesive explanation of the underlying dynamics of certain aspects of behavior. For example, self-verification theory indicates that people attempt to maintain stable self-concepts. Based on this theory, we can make a number of predictions. For instance, if the theory is correct, we might predict that people with poor self-concepts will seek out negative social reinforcement (e.g., seek out people who give them negative feedback about themselves) while avoiding or rejecting positive reinforcement.[1] Such predictions can be tested with empirical research,

---

[1] For more information on this theory, see Joiner, T. E., Katz, J., & Lew, A. S. (1997). Self-verification and depression among youth psychiatric inpatients. *Journal of Abnormal Psychology*, *106*, 608-618. Also see Swann, Jr., W. B., Stein-Seroussi, A., & Giesler, R. B. (1992). Why people self-verify. *Journal of Personality and Social Psychology*, *62*, 392-401.

which sheds light on the validity of a theory as well as data that may be used to further develop and refine it.

In addition to testing whether the predictions made on the basis of a theory are supported by data, researchers conduct studies to determine under what circumstances the elements of a theory hold up (e.g., In intimate relationships only? With mildly as well as severely depressed patients?). One researcher might test one aspect of the theory with a convenience sample of adolescent boys who are being treated for depression, another might test a different aspect with a convenience sample of high-achieving women, and so on. Note that they are focusing on the theory as an evolving concept rather than as a static explanation that needs to be tested with a random sample for generalization to a population. These studies may be viewed as *developmental tests* of a theory. For preliminary developmental work of this type, rigorous and expensive sampling from large populations is usually not justified.

3. Some researchers prefer to study a *purposive sample*, rather than a random one. A purposive sample is one in which a researcher has a special interest because its members have characteristics that make them an especially rich source of information. For example, an anthropologist who is interested in studying tribal religious practices might purposively select a tribe that has remained isolated and, hence, may have been less influenced by outside religions than other tribes that are less isolated. Note that the tribe is not selected at random but is selected deliberately (i.e., purposively). The use of purposive samples is a tradition in *qualitative* research. (If you have not done so already, see Appendix A for a brief overview of the differences between qualitative and quantitative research.)

4. Some researchers study entire populations—not samples. This is especially true in institutional settings such as schools where all the seniors in a school district (the population) might be tested. Nevertheless, when researchers write research reports on population studies, they should describe their populations in some detail.

___ 1. Has the researcher described the sample/population in sufficient detail?

Comment: As you know from the previous chapter, researchers should describe relevant demographics (i.e., background characteristics) of their participants when conducting studies in which they are generalizing from a sample to a population. This is also true when researchers are not attempting to generalize. For example, if a published pilot study shows promise for collecting meaningful data on safe sex practices among high school students, the reader will want to know exactly what types of students were selected as participants. Were they high-achieving, articulate students? If so, the data collection procedures may not work as well with lower-achieving students. Were their parents highly educated? If so, obtaining parental permission to participate in such a study might be more difficult when the parents are less well educated. Answers to such questions are important because the role of a pilot study is to lay the groundwork for later, more definitive studies with samples more suitable for generalizing to a population.

Example 7.1.1 is drawn from a report on a developmental test of two theories. Based on each theory, an HIV risk reduction intervention was developed and tested in an experiment. The example shows a brief but solid description of relevant demographics of the sample.

Example 7.1.1[2]

Detailed description of relevant characteristics of participants:

Incarcerated women ($N = 90$) were recruited from a state women's prison near a southern city with a population of approximately 400,000 and an AIDS incidence of 15.4 per 100,000 (CDC, 1995). Approximately one-third of the women were incarcerated for drug offenses and a further one-third were incarcerated for drug-related offenses (e.g., burglary to procure money for drugs). Thirteen percent (13%) reported self-injecting with needle sharing, and 25% reported using crack cocaine in the preceding year. Participants were between the ages of 17 and 53 ($M = 31.6$ years, $SD = 7.7$) and averaged 10.9 years of education ($SD = 2.4$). Household income in the preceding year was less than $10,000 per year for 85.7% of the sample and below $20,000 for 96.3%. Approximately one-third of the sample was married (35.0%), and the average number of children was 2.4 ($SD = 1.7$). Conjugal visits were allowed for the married inmates. Most of the women were African American (80.7%), and the rest were White (19.3%), consistent with the racial demographics of the prison. The mean number of lifetime sex partners reported was 21.6 ($SD = 38.9$; range, 0–300) and 43.8% had been treated for a sexually transmitted disease.

___ 2. For a pilot study or developmental test of a theory, has the researcher used a sample with relevant demographics?

Comment: Studies that often fail on this evaluation question are those in which college students are used as participants (for convenience in sampling). For example, some researchers have gotten far afield by conducting studies in which college students are asked to respond to questions that are unrelated to their life experiences such as asking unmarried, childless college women what disciplinary measures they would take if they discovered that their hypothetical teenage sons were using illicit drugs. Obviously, this would yield little relevant information in a pilot study of a questionnaire designed for use with actual parents of teenagers.

---

[2] St. Lawrence, J. S., Eldridge, G. D., Shelby, M. C., Little, C. E., Brasfield, T. L., & O'Bannon, R. E. (1997). HIV risk reduction for incarcerated women: A comparison of brief interventions based on two theoretical models. *Journal of Consulting and Clinical Psychology, 65,* 504-509.

Less absurd examples abound in the published literature such as using college students in tests of learning theories when the theories were constructed to explain the learning behavior of children. When applying this evaluation question to such studies, you should make some allowance for a "misfit" between the sample used in the pilot study (or developmental test of a theory) and the population of ultimate interest. Keep in mind that these types of studies are not designed to provide definitive data—only preliminary information that will assist in refining future research.

___ 3. Even if the purpose is not to generalize to a population, has the researcher used a sample of adequate size?

Comment: Very preliminary studies might be conducted using exceedingly small samples such as trying out a questionnaire with only a handful of participants. While such studies might be useful to the researcher, their results are usually not publishable. Because there are no scientific standards for what constitutes a reasonable sample size for a pilot study to be publishable, you will need to make subjective judgments when answering this evaluation question. Likewise, there are no standards for sample sizes for developmental tests of theory.

For purposive samples, which are common in qualitative research, the sample size may be determined by the availability of participants who fit the sampling profile for the purposive sample. For instance, to study the career paths of highly achieving women in education, a researcher might decide to use female directors of statewide education agencies. If there are only a handful of such women, the sample will necessarily be limited to that number. On the other hand, when there are many potential participants who meet the standards for a purposive sample, a researcher might continue contacting additional participants until the point of "saturation," that is, the point at which additional participants are adding little new to the picture that is emerging. In other words, new participants are revealing the same types of information as those who have already participated. Example 7.3.1 illustrates how this was described in a study of high school dropouts in which researchers interviewed dropouts to identify reasons for dropping out.

Example 7.3.1[3]
A statement justifying the use of a small purposive sample:

The study stopped when the school stories of 12 families had been collected. Why this number? Because, as we will demonstrate in the

---

[3] Okey, T. N. & Cusick, P. A. (1995). Dropping out: Another side of the story. *Educational Administration Quarterly, 31*, 244-267.

ensuing explanation, the same story kept coming up again and again. The categories that emerged with the first family—economic problems, risk factors, disinterest in academics, trouble with authorities—were, by the 12th family, fully saturated. No new categories arose.

___ **4. If a purposive sample has been used, has the researcher indicated the basis for selecting individuals to include?**

Comment: Researchers should indicate the basis or criteria for the selection of a purposive sample as illustrated in Example 7.4.1, which is taken from a qualitative study on art education for the gifted.

Example 7.4.1[4]

A description of the basis for selecting a purposive sample:

Criteria for site selection included conditions such as the presence of an ongoing artistically gifted program and a school district with administrative and community history of support for gifted and talented programming. The researcher selected the school district because it was one of the first in the state to act as a model site for gifted programs, initiating artistically gifted programs along with academic ones. The selected program began in 1987 as a pilot program for the school district.

Note that even if a researcher calls his or her sample "purposive," it should usually be regarded as merely a sample of convenience unless the basis for its selection is described.

___ **5. If a population has been studied, has it been clearly identified and described?**

Comment: Researchers who conduct population studies often disguise the true identity of their populations (for ethical and legal reasons), especially if the results reflect negatively on the population. Nevertheless, information should be given that helps the reader visualize the population, as illustrated in Example 7.5.1. Notice that the specific city is not mentioned, but relevant information is given. Also note that "all social workers" constitutes a population.

---

[4]Wolfe, P. (1997). A really good art teacher would be like you, Mrs. C.: A qualitative study of a teacher and her artistically gifted middle school students. *Studies in Art Education, 38,* 232-245.

Example 7.5.1
Description of a population that was studied:

All social workers in a medium-size city in the southeast were interviewed. All were college graduates with 11% holding master's degrees while the rest had bachelor's degrees. The average age (median) was 39.4. The self-reported ethnicity/racial groups were White (62%), African American (30%) and "decline to state" (8%). The average salary adjusted for education and years on the job ($41,200) was slightly above the regional average.

With information such as that provided in the example, readers can make educated judgments as to whether the results are likely to apply to other populations of social workers.

___ 6. Has the researcher obtained informed consent?

Comment: This evaluation was raised in the previous chapter on evaluating samples when researchers generalize. (See Evaluation Question 11 in Chapter 6.) It is being raised again in this chapter because it applies whether researchers are attempting to generalize or not.

___ 7. Overall, is the description of the sample adequate?

Comment: Rate this evaluation question after considering your answers to the earlier ones in this chapter and any additional considerations and concerns you may have. Be prepared to rewrite the abstracts of research reports to which you assign low ratings.

Exercise for Chapter 7

Directions: Locate several research reports of interest to you in academic journals in which the researchers are not directly concerned with generalizing from a sample to a population, and apply the evaluation questions in this chapter. Select the one to which you gave the highest overall rating and bring it to class for discussion. Be prepared to discuss its strengths and weaknesses.

Chapter 8

Evaluating Instrumentation

Immediately after describing the sample or population they studied, researchers almost always describe their *instruments*. An instrument is any tool or method for measuring a trait or characteristic. The description of instruments is usually identified with the subheading *Instrumentation*.[1]

Often, researchers use previously published instruments developed by others. These are easy to spot because their titles will be capitalized and references for them will be given. Perhaps equally often, researchers use instruments that they devise specifically for their particular research purposes. As a general rule, researchers should provide more information about such newly developed measures than on previously published instruments that have been described in detail in other publications such as test manuals and research reports.

While you would need to take several sequential courses in measurement to become an expert, you will be able to make first-blush evaluations of researchers' measurement procedures by applying the evaluation questions given below. Of course, your evaluations will be more definitive if you have first taken a measurement course or studied the chapter(s) on measurement in your research methods textbook.

____ **1. Have the actual items, questions, and/or directions (or, at least, a sample of them) been provided?**

Comment: Providing sample items, questions, or directions is highly desirable because they help to operationalize what was measured. Note that researchers *operationalize* when they specify the physical properties of the concepts on which they are reporting.

In Example 8.1.1, the researchers provide samples of the actual questions they asked fourth-grade students in their study. Notice that by providing actual questions, readers of the research are in a position to evaluate the suitability of the questions for use with the participants. For example, the simple statements in the instrument and the use of "old people" instead of "elderly" make it likely that the fourth-grade students in this study would be able to comprehend them.

---

[1] As you know from Chapter 1, *observation* is a broad term that encompasses all forms of *measurement*. The term *instrumentation* refers to the materials and tests that are used to make the observations or obtain the measurements.

Example 8.1.1[2]
Sample inventory questions administered to fourth graders:

One measure used was the Children's Perceptions of Aging and Elderly (CPAE) inventory…. The instrument contained 20 items…. Participants expressed their agreement or disagreement with each statement on a Likert-type scale. Items include statements such as "Old people are not very smart." "Old people are very intelligent." "Old people are sick all the time."

In Example 8.1.2, the researcher provides the wording of an interview question that was posed to adults in a national survey. Notice that the question includes a definition of "affirmative action," which was done to ensure that the respondents all had a common understanding of what it is. Also note that by being given the actual words, readers of the research can evaluate the adequacy of the definition as well as other aspects of the question such as the difficulty of the vocabulary used.

Example 8.1.2[3]
Sample interview question given:

"As you know, some affirmative action programs are designed to give preferential treatment to women/racial minorities in such areas as getting jobs and promotions, obtaining contracts, and being admitted to schools. Do you generally approve or disapprove of affirmative action programs?"

Keep in mind that some instruments are copyrighted and their copyright holders might insist on keeping the actual items secure from public exposure. Obviously, a researcher should not be faulted for failing to provide samples when this is the case. In addition, you may want to make allowances on this evaluation question when a researcher has used a published test that is widely known and used in his or her field. Researchers who use such instruments may believe that it is not necessary to provide samples from them. Generally, the failure to supply sample items is less of a flaw when the instrument is well-known than when it is newly developed.

[2] Aday, R. H., Sims, C. R., McDuffie, W., & Evans, E. (1996). Changing children's attitudes toward the elderly: The longitudinal effects of an intergenerational partners program. *Journal of Research in Childhood Education, 10*, 143–151.
[3] Moore, D. W. (1995). Americans today are dubious about affirmative action. *The Gallup Poll Monthly*, (No. 354), 36–38.

___ 2. Are any specialized response formats and/or restrictions described in detail?

Comment: If a researcher has provided samples of the actual items, questions, or directions, the response format may already be clear. If not, it is desirable to describe how participants were expected to respond, as illustrated in Example 8.2.1 in which researchers give a reference for the instrument, present a sample item, and describe the response format (i.e., Likert scale).

Example 8.2.1[4]
Excerpt that includes a description of the response format for an instrument:

We assessed this variable [parent's self-reported job insecurity] with Kuhnert and Vance's (1992) 18-item job insecurity measure. Respondents rated all 18 items (e.g., "I can be sure of my present job as long as I do good work"; reverse coded) on a 5-point Likert scale (1 = *strongly disagree*; 5 = *strongly agree*).... High scores reflect job insecurity.

In addition to response formats, other conditions or restrictions should be described. Examples are: "Participants were instructed not to discuss their responses with each other until the end of the study" and "Because of the young age of the participants, interviews were limited to 15 minutes or less and interviewers were instructed to conclude an interview as quickly as possible if a child became very restless or distracted."

___ 3. For published instruments, have sources where additional information can be obtained been cited?

Comment: Some instruments are "published" only in the sense that they were reproduced in full in journal articles. Such articles typically describe the development and statistical properties of the instrument. Others are published by test publishers as separate publications (e.g., test booklets) that usually have accompanying manuals that describe technical information on the instruments. References to these published sources allow a fuller evaluation of the instrument by those who are working intensely in an area such as dissertation students.

In Example 8.3.1, the researchers briefly describe a scale by giving a reference to a book in which it was described in detail by its author (i.e., Zuckerman, 1979) as well as two other sources of published information.

---

[4] Barling, J., Dupre, K. E., & Hepburn, C. G. (1998). Effects of parents' job insecurity on children's work beliefs and attitudes. *Journal of Applied Psychology, 83,* 112-118.

Example 8.3.1[5]

The description of an instrument in which references are given:

This 10-item subscale of the Sensation Seeking Scales, Form V (Zuckerman, 1979), was used as one measure of alcoholism and alcohol abuse risk…(see Zuckerman, 1979 for an in-depth discussion…). This measure has been reliably associated with alcohol use and risk, especially in college students, although problems with criterion contamination may exist (Darkes, Greenbaum, & Goldman, in press; La Grange, Jones, Erb, & Reyes, 1995).

___ 4. When delving into sensitive matters, is there reason to believe that accurate data were obtained?

Comment: Some issues are sensitive because they deal with illegal matters such as illicit substance use, gang violence, and so on. Others are sensitive because of societal taboos such as those regarding certain forms of sexual behavior. Still others may be sensitive because of idiosyncratic personal views on privacy. For instance, age and income are sensitive issues for many individuals; they often decline to answer questions about them or may not answer honestly.

A basic technique for encouraging honest answers to sensitive questions is to collect the responses anonymously. For instance, participants may be asked to mail in questionnaires with the assurance that they are not coded in any way that would reveal their identity. In group settings, participants may also be assured that their responses are anonymous, but if a group is small, such as a class of 20 students, some participants might be hesitant to be perfectly honest regarding highly sensitive matters because a small group does not provide much "cover" for hiding the identity of a participant who engages in illegal or taboo behaviors.

With some techniques such as interviewing or direct physical observation, it is not possible to provide anonymity. The most a researcher might be able to do is to assure *confidentiality*. Such an assurance is likely to work best if the participants already know and trust the interviewer (such as a school counselor) or if the researcher has spent enough time with the participants to develop rapport and trust. The latter is more likely to occur in qualitative research than quantitative research because qualitative researchers often spend substantial amounts of time getting to know and interacting with their participants.

---

[5] Darkes, J. & Goldman, M. S. (1998). Expectancy challenge and drinking reduction process and structure in the alcohol expectancy network. *Experimental and Clinical Psychopharmacology, 6,* 64-76.

___ 5. Have steps been taken to keep the instrumentation from obtruding on and changing any overt behaviors that were observed?

Comment: If participants know they are being directly observed, they may temporarily change their behavior. Clearly, this is likely to happen when studying highly sensitive behaviors, but it can also affect data collection on more ordinary matters. For instance, some students may suddenly be on their best behavior if one day they come to class to find a video camera focused on them; other students may show off by acting out under such circumstances.

One solution would be to make surreptitious observations such as with a hidden video camera or by using a one-way mirror. In many circumstances, such techniques may raise serious ethical problems.

Another solution is to make the observational procedures a routine part of the research setting. For instance, if it is routine for a classroom to be visited frequently by outsiders (e.g., parents, school staff, and university observers), the presence of a researcher may be unlikely to obtrude on the behavior of the students.

___ 6. If the collection and coding of observations is highly subjective, is there evidence that similar results would be obtained if another researcher used the same measurement techniques with the same group at the same time?

Comment: Suppose a researcher observes groups of adolescent males interacting in various public settings, such as shopping malls, in order to collect data on aggressive behavior. Identifying some aggressive behaviors may require considerable subjectivity. If an adolescent puffs out his chest, is this a threatening behavior or merely a manifestation of a big sigh of relief? Is a scowl a sign of aggression or merely an expression of unhappiness? Answering such questions requires some subjectivity.

An important technique for addressing this issue is to have two or more independent observers make observations of the same participants at the same time. If the *rate of agreement* on the identification and classification of the behavior is reasonably high (say, 70% or more), a consumer of research will be assured that the resulting data are not idiosyncratic to one particular observer and his or her powers of observation and possible biases.

The rate of agreement is sometimes referred to as *interobserver reliability*. When the observations are reduced to scores for each participant (such as a total score for nonverbal aggressiveness), the scores based on two independent observers' observations can be expressed as an *interobserver reliability coefficient.* In reliability studies, these can range from 0.00 to 1.00 with coefficients of about 0.70 or higher indicating adequate interobserver reliability.[6]

___ 7. If an instrument is designed to measure a single unitary trait, does it have adequate internal consistency?

Comment: A test of computational skills in mathematics at the primary grade level measures a relatively homogeneous trait. However, a mathematics battery that measures verbal problem-solving and mathematical reasoning in addition to computational skills measures a more heterogeneous trait. Likewise, a self-report measure of cheerfulness measures a more homogenous trait than a measure of overall mental health does.

For instruments designed to measure homogenous traits, it is important to ask whether they are *internally consistent*, that is, to what extent are the items within the instrument consistent with each other in terms of what they measure? While it is beyond the scope of this book to explain how and why it works, a statistic known as Cronbach's alpha (whose symbol is α) provides a statistical measure of internal consistency. As a special type of correlation coefficient, it ranges from 0.00 to 1.00 with values of about 0.70 or above indicating adequate internal consistency.[7] Values below this suggest that more than one trait is being measured by the instrument, which is undesirable when a researcher wants to measure only one homogenous trait.

Examples 8.7.1 and 8.7.2 illustrate typical statements in research reports concerning this issue. Note that internal consistency is regarded by many as a specialized type of reliability, hence the use of the term *reliability* in Example 8.7.2. Other forms of reliability are discussed under Evaluation Question 8 below.

Internal consistency is usually regarded as an issue only when an instrument is designed to measure a single homogeneous trait *and* when the instrument yields scores (as opposed to instruments such as interviews when used to identify patterns that are described in words). If an instrument does not meet these two criteria, you should answer "not applicable" to this evaluation question.

---

[6] Mathematically, these coefficients are the same as *correlation coefficients*, which are covered in all standard introductory statistics courses. You may know that correlation coefficients can range from –1.00 to 1.00, with a value of 0.00 indicating no relationship. In practice, however, negatives are not found in reliability studies.

[7] *Split-half reliability* also measures internal consistency, but Cronbach's alpha is widely considered a superior measure. Hence, split-half reliability is seldom reported. Should you encounter it, it will be expressed as a coefficient with values of about 0.70 and above being considered satisfactory.

Example 8.7.1[8]

Statement regarding internal consistency identified as α:

The ten items of the Depressive Symptoms Severity Index (DSSI; $\alpha = .87$) cover depressed mood, lack of interest or pleasure in daily activities, fatigue or loss of energy...

Example 8.7.2[9]

Statement regarding internal consistency identified as "reliability" and as "Cronbach's alpha":

Reliability of the Aggression and Victimization scales was satisfactory. Cronbach's alpha coefficients for the fall (and spring) assessments of aggression and victimization, respectively, were .85 (.81) and .87 (.87).

____ 8. For stable traits, is there evidence of temporal stability?

Comment: Suppose a researcher wants to measure aptitude (i.e., potential or ability) for learning algebra. Such an aptitude is widely regarded as being stable. In other words, it is unlikely to fluctuate much from one week or even one year to another without additional mathematics instruction. Hence, a test of such an aptitude should yield results that are stable across at least short periods of time. To put it more concretely, if a student's score on such a test administered this week indicates that he or she has very little aptitude for learning algebra, this test should yield a similar assessment if administered to the same student next week.

Although it is a little harder to see, most measures of personality also should yield results that have temporal stability (i.e., are stable over time). For example, suppose a researcher wants to measure the deep-seated, long-term self-esteem of participants. While self-esteem may fluctuate modestly over even short periods of time, a researcher usually does *not* want a measure that is overly sensitive to such temporary fluctuations. Hence, he or she would want to use a measure that yields scores that are similar from one week or one month to another.

The most straightforward approach to assessing temporal stability is to administer the instrument to a group of participants twice at different points in time—typically with a couple of weeks between administrations, although sometimes it is examined over a more extended period of time. The two sets of scores can be correlated and if a coefficient of about 0.70 or more (on a scale

---

[8] Moos, R. H., Cronkite, R. C., & Moos, B. S. (1998). The long-term interplay between family and extrafamily resources and depression. *Journal of Family Psychology, 12,* 326-343.
[9] Egan, S. K., Monson, T. C., & Perry, D. G. (1998). Social-cognitive influences on change in aggression over time. *Developmental Psychology, 5,* 996-1006.

from 0.00 to 1.00) is obtained, there is evidence of temporal stability. This type of reliability is commonly known as *test-retest reliability*. As its name implies, this type of reliability is usually examined only when *tests* or scales that yield scores are used in research.

While temporal stability is an important issue, it is usually addressed in research reports mainly when researchers use previously published instruments that have been extensively studied. Unfortunately, researchers seldom examine temporal stability when using instruments newly developed for use in a particular study on which they are reporting, since establishing temporal reliability would constitute a study in and of itself.

Example 8.8.1 illustrates how researchers describe what is known about the temporal stability of a previously published test they used.

Example 8.8.1[10]

Statement regarding temporal stability (test-retest reliability):

The State-Trait Inventory (STAI; Spielberger, 1983) is one of the most widely used measures of anxiety for clinical assessment and research. The Trait scale of the STAI measures the degree of past anxiety and present proneness to anxiety…. Test-retest reliability estimates ranged from .65 to .77 over 30-, 60-, and 104-day periods.

___ 9. When appropriate, is there evidence of content validity?

Comment: An important issue in the evaluation of achievement tests is the extent to which the contents of the tests (i.e., the stimulus materials and skills) are suitable in light of the research purpose. For instance, if a researcher has used an achievement test to study the extent to which the second graders in a school district have achieved the skills expected of them at this grade level, an evaluator of the research will want to know whether the contents of the test are aligned with (or match) the contents of the second-grade curriculum.

While content validity is most closely associated with measurement of achievement, it is also sometimes used as a construct for evaluating other types of measures. For instance, a researcher might point out that the contents of a scale designed to measure depression correspond to a list of traits associated with depression outlined in a widely accepted diagnostic manual on psychological disorders. Such a match assures readers of the research that the measure of depression represents mainstream thinking regarding this trait.[11]

---

[10] Lee, R. M. & Robbins, S. B. (1998). The relationship between social connectedness and anxiety, self-esteem, and social identity. *Journal of Counseling Psychology, 3*, 338-345.

[11] Of course, some researchers deviate from the mainstream on certain measurement issues. There is nothing inherently wrong with this as long as the deviation(s) are clearly described and a rationale is given for them.

____ 10. When appropriate, is there evidence of empirical validity?

Comment: Empirical validity refers to validity established by collecting data using the instrument in order to determine the extent to which the data "make sense." For instance, a depression scale might be empirically validated by administering it to an institutionalized, clinically depressed group of adult patients as well as to a random sample of adult patients visiting family physicians for annual checkups. We would expect that the scores of the two groups will differ substantially in a predicted direction (i.e., the institutionalized sample should have higher depression scores). If not, the validity of the scale would be quite questionable.

Sometimes the empirical validity of a test is expressed with a correlation coefficient. For example, a test maker might correlate scores on the College Board's SAT with freshman grades in college. A correlation of .40 or more might be interpreted as indicating the test has validity as a modest predictor of college grades.

Empirical validity comes in many forms, and a full exploration of it would require a book of its own. Some key terms that suggest that empirical validity has been explored are *predictive validity, concurrent validity, criterion-related validity, discriminate validity, construct validity,* and *factor analysis.*

If you are new to the field of research and measurement, you may feel at this point that you would be hopelessly lost in trying to evaluate instruments in light of this evaluation question. However, you can check to see whether a researcher has addressed this issue. When researchers do this, they usually only briefly summarize the information, and these summaries are usually comprehensible to those who have minimal training in measurement and statistics. Examples 8.10.1 and 8.10.2 illustrate fairly typical summaries. Notice that they are exceptionally brief but contain references to publications where additional information may be obtained.

Example 8.10.1[12]

Statement regarding empirical validity of an instrument with a reference to its test manual[13] where more information may be obtained:

The Test of Early Reading Ability-2 (TERS-2) (Reid, Hresko, & Hammill, 1989) is a norm-referenced assessment instrument.... The authors reported adequate construct validity including significant correlations (.61) with performance on the Basic Skills Inventory-Diagnostic Reading Subtest, high correlations with chronological age and

---

[12] Sacks, C. H. & Mergendoller, J. R. (1997). The relationship between teachers' theoretical orientation toward reading and student outcomes in kindergarten children with different initial reading abilities. *American Educational Research Journal, 34,* 721–739.

[13] Note that the reference to Reid, Hresko, & Hammill, 1989, is a reference to the manual for the test.

school experience (.84), and successful differentiation of normal and learning-disabled students.

Example 8.10.2[14]

Statement regarding empirical validity of an instrument with a reference where more information may be obtained:

The Male Role Norms Scale (MRNS) is a 26-item self-report scale consisting of statements about male role norms and behaviors.... Evidence of construct validity has been established by positive relations with masculine gender role stress (see Thompson, Pleck, & Ferrera, 1992).

Unfortunately, empirical validity is seldom addressed when researchers use newly developed instruments devised for their specific research studies. This is because an adequate empirical validity study is a major study in and of itself.

Note that it is traditional for researchers to address empirical validity only for instruments that yield scores, as opposed to instruments such as semistructured interviews.

___ 11. Is the instrumentation adequate in light of the research purpose?

Comment: One of the most important things you can do when evaluating instrumentation is to consider it in light of a researcher's purpose for conducting a study. Is there a match between what the researcher needs to measure to achieve his or her purpose and the instrument he or she selected?

Careful researchers attempt to show their readers that they have selected instruments appropriate for achieving their research objectives. Often, they will discuss why a particular instrument was chosen over others or how an instrument was modified to make it more suitable to the research purpose. This is illustrated in Example 8.11.1 in which the researchers modified a scale to make it suitable for use with both the Japanese and Australian students in their study.

---

[14] Tokar, D. M. & Jome, L. M. (1998). Masculinity, vocational interests, and career choice traditionality: Evidence for a fully mediated model. *Journal of Counseling Psychology, 45,* 424–435.

Example 8.11.1[15]

Statement in which the researcher discusses the rationale for selecting and the modification of an instrument for a particular research project:

The Self-Regulated Learning Interview Schedule (Zimmerman & Martinez-Pons, 1986, 1988, 1990) was used as the basis for the construction of a written survey of students' learning strategies. In the survey, students were presented with a number of different vignettes.... Preliminary interviews were conducted with three native Japanese students who...were familiar with both the Japanese and the Australian secondary school learning environments. Discussions with two bilingual, bicultural teachers...were also conducted. The purpose of these discussions was to confirm that the contexts described in the learning vignettes would hold the same meaning for both Australian and Japanese students and that they were realistic representations of the sorts of learning activities typically engaged in by Japanese students in Japanese schools. On the basis of these interviews, several modifications were made to the vignettes originally developed by Zimmerman and Martinez-Pons (1986, 1988, 1990).

Of course, not all researchers find it necessary to modify an instrument. However, from whatever information a researcher does provide, you should make a judgment as to the suitability of the instrument in light of the research purpose.

___ 12. Overall, is the instrumentation adequate?

Comment: Example 8.12.1 shows the types of information you might expect to find on an instrument. A statement regarding statistical properties of an instrument such as the one in the second paragraph in the example is more likely to appear in the description of a previously published instrument (especially one that yields scores) than in the description of a newly developed one.

---

[15] Purdie, N. & Hattie, J. (1996). Cultural differences in the use of strategies for self-regulated learning. *American Educational Research Journal, 33,* 845–871.

Example 8.12.1[16]

A complete statement regarding an instrument used in a study whose purpose was to examine theoretical relationships among predictors of higher-level career aspirations among college women:

Seven items developed by Lips (1992) were used to assess students' beliefs in the compatibility of science careers with marriage and family responsibilities for women. Respondents rated, on a 5-point Likert-type scale (1 = *strongly disagree* to 5 = *strongly agree*), their agreement with statements reflecting attitudes about the possibility of women successfully combining career and family responsibilities. Sample items include: "It is very difficult for a woman to combine a career as a scientist with a family life," "If a woman scientist or engineer takes time away from her career to have children, she will never catch up again," and "For women, there is nothing incompatible about planning both a family and a top-level scientific or engineering career" (reverse scored). Possible average scores ranged from 1 to 5, with lower scores representing more positive attitudes about the possibility of combining science career and family responsibilities.

Lips (1992) reported a reliability coefficient of .75 for this set of items. Cronbach's alpha for the seven items in this study was .81. Support for the items' validity was indicated by a positive relationship between scale scores and female students' selection of science-related academic and vocational goals (Lips, 1992).

As you can see in the above example, the statistical information is quite brief. It is unrealistic to expect extensive technical information on all instruments used in research because it is traditional to be brief on this matter, especially if there are other published sources where this information can be obtained.

Note that sometimes an instrument will simply appear valid on its face without statistical reliability and validity data. When reporting on a survey on attitudes toward affirmative action, for example, the researcher may simply provide you with the actual wording of the questions used with no additional information. You may decide that this is sufficient for you to evaluate the adequacy of the instrumentation.

In reaching your overall evaluation, you should usually place more emphasis on Evaluation Question 11 "Is the instrumentation adequate in light of the research purpose?" than on the other questions. This is because an instrument that passes muster on all the other questions but fails Question 11 is

---

[16] Nauta, M. M., Epperson, D. L., & Kahn, J. H. (1998). A multiple-groups analysis of predictors of higher level career aspirations among women in mathematics, science, and engineering majors. *Journal of Counseling Psychology, 45,* 483–496.

invalid for use in the particular research you are considering. For example, if a researcher needs to measure reading comprehension to achieve his or her research purpose, but for the sake of expediency uses a test that is known to be a highly valid and reliable measure of vocabulary knowledge (one limited aspect of reading comprehension), the test has limited validity *for this particular research purpose.* In other words, validity is relative to the purpose for which an instrument is being used. It might be highly valid for one purpose but have limited validity for another. Likewise, it is relative to the backgrounds of the participants. For example, a measure that works well with children might have less validity with adults.

Generally speaking, if a researcher provides too little information for you to make an informed judgment, you should give it a low rating on this evaluation question.

Exercise for Chapter 8

Directions: Locate several research reports of interest to you in academic journals. Evaluate the descriptions of the instruments in light of the evaluation questions in this chapter as well as any other considerations and concerns you may have. Select the one to which you gave the highest overall rating and bring it to class for discussion. Be prepared to discuss both its strengths and weaknesses.

Notes:

Chapter 9

Evaluating Experimental Procedures

An experiment is a study in which treatments are given in order to determine their effects. For example, we might train one group of children how to use conflict-resolution techniques (the experimental group) and compare them with another group of children who are not trained (the control group). Following this, we could observe all the children on the playground to determine whether the experimental group used more conflict-resolution techniques than the control group did.

The treatments (training versus no training) constitute what is known as the *independent variable*, which can be thought of as the stimulus or input variable. The resulting behavior on the playground constitutes the *dependent variable*, which can be thought of as the output or response variable.

You will be able to spot experiments because any study in which even a single treatment is given to even a single participant is an experiment as long as the purpose of the study is to determine the effects of the treatment(s) on another variable. A study that does not meet these minimal conditions is *not* an experiment. Thus, for example, a political poll in which questions are asked but no treatments are given is not an experiment and should not be referred to as such.

The following evaluation questions cover only the most important principles for the evaluation of experiments. To a large extent, the presentation is nontechnical. To become conversant with the technical terms and jargon associated with experimentation, consult any major research methods textbook.

____ 1. **If two or more groups are compared, were individuals assigned at random to the groups?**

Comment: By assigning individuals at random to the groups, we are assured that there is no bias in the assignment. For example, random assignment to two groups in the experiment on conflict-resolution training (mentioned at the beginning of this chapter) assures us that there is no bias such as systematically assigning the less aggressive children to the experimental group. It is *not* safe to assume the assignment was at random unless a researcher explicitly states that it was, which is done in Example 9.1.1.

Example 9.1.1[1]

Excerpt from an experiment, random assignment explicitly mentioned:

Thirty-five male and 49 female (predominantely Caucasian) introductory psychology students participated in the experiment to fulfill a course requirement. The subjects were primarily first-year students and were randomly assigned to conditions.

Note that assigning *individuals* to treatments at random is vastly superior to assigning previously existing groups to treatments at random. For example, in educational research, it is not uncommon to assign one class to an experimental treatment and another class to serve as the control group. Because students are not ordinarily randomly assigned to classes, there may be systematic differences between the two classes. School principals and counselors use various criteria and considerations in making class assignments, and these can be presumed to lead to the creation of groups that are systematically different. Thus, you should *not* answer "yes" to this evaluation question unless *individuals* were assigned at random.

If you can answer "yes" to this evaluation question, the experiment you are evaluating is known as a *true experiment*. Note that this term does not imply that the experiment is perfect, as you will see as you apply some of the other evaluation questions in this chapter.

___ **2. If two or more comparison groups were *not* formed at random, is there evidence that they were initially equal in important ways?**

Comment: Suppose a researcher wants to study the impact of a new third-grade reading program that is being used with all third graders in a school (the experimental group). To get a control group, he or she will have to use third graders in another school.[2] Because students are not randomly assigned to schools, this experiment will get low marks on Evaluation Question 1. However, if the researcher selects a control school in which the first graders have standardized test scores similar to those in the experimental school and are similar in other important respects such as parents' socioeconomic status, some useful information may still be obtained.

Note, however, that having such evidence of similarity between groups is not as satisfactory as assigning individuals at random to groups. For example, the children in the two schools in our example may be different in some

---

[1] Johnson, J. D. (1994). The effect of rape type and information admissibility on perceptions of rape victims. *Sex Roles, 30,* 781–792.

[2] As you may know, the use of two intact groups (groups that were already formed) with both a pretest and a posttest is known as a *quasi-experiment*—as opposed to a true experiment.

important respect that the researcher has overlooked. Perhaps the children's parents in the experimental school are more involved in their children's schooling than the parents in the other school. This involvement, rather than the new reading program, might be the cause of any differences in reading achievement between the two groups.

When using two intact groups (such as two schools), it is important to give both a pretest and a posttest to measure the dependent variable. For instance, to evaluate the reading program, a researcher should give a pretest in reading, which will establish whether the two intact groups are initially similar on the dependent variable. Of course, the experiment will be more interpretable if they are initially similar.[3]

___ 3. If only a single participant or a single group is used, have the treatments been alternated?

Comment: Not all experiments involve the comparison of groups that have been treated differently. Consider, for example, a teacher who wants to try using increased praise for appropriate behaviors in the classroom to see if it reduces inappropriate behaviors such as inappropriate out-of-seat behavior (IOSB). To conduct an experiment on this, he or she could count the number of IOSBs for a week or two before administering the increased praise. This would yield what is called the *baseline data*. Suppose the teacher then introduces the extra praise and finds a decrease in the IOSBs. This might suggest that the extra praise *caused* the improvement. However, such a conclusion would be highly tenuous because children's environments are constantly changing in many ways and some other environmental influence (such as the school principal scolding the students on the playground without the teacher's knowledge) might be the real cause of the change. A more definitive test would be for the teacher to reverse the treatment and go back to giving less praise, followed by another reversal to the higher praise condition. If the data form the expected pattern, the teacher would have reasonable evidence that increased praise reduces IOSB.

Notice that in this type of experiment, the single group serves as a control during the baseline, serves as the experimental group when the extra praise is initially given, serves as the control again when the condition is reversed, and finally serves as the experimental group again when the extra praise is reintroduced. Such a design has this strength: The same children with the same backgrounds are both the experimental and control groups. (In a two-group

---

[3] If the groups are initially dissimilar, a researcher should consider locating another group that is more similar to serve as the control. If this is not possible, a statistical technique known as analysis of covariance can be used to adjust the posttest scores in light of the initial differences in pretest scores. Such a statistical adjustment can be risky if the assumptions underlying the test have been violated, a topic beyond the scope of this book.

experiment, the children in one group may be different from the children in the other group in some important way that affects the outcome of the experiment.) The major drawback of a single group design is that the same children are being exposed to multiple treatments, which may lead to unnatural reactions. How does a child feel when some weeks he or she gets extra praise for appropriate behaviors but other weeks does not? Obviously, such reactions could confound the experiment.

If two classes wcrc available for an experiment of the type we are considering, a teacher could use a *multiple baseline design*, in which the initial extra praise condition is started on a different week for each group. If the pattern of decreased IOSB under the extra praise condition holds up across both groups, the causal conclusion would be even stronger than when only one group was used at one point in time.

The type of experimentation being discussed under this evaluation question is often referred to as *single-subject research* or *behavior analysis*. When a professional has only a single participant or intact group that cannot be divided at random into two groups, such a design can provide useful information about causality.

___ 4. Are the treatments described in sufficient detail?

Comment: Researchers should give rather thorough descriptions of the treatments that were administered since the sole purpose of an experiment is to estimate the effects of the treatments on dependent variables. The reader should be able to picture what was done and by whom. If the treatments are complex such as two types of therapy in clinical psychology applied for an extended period of time, researchers should give references to additional publications where detailed accounts can be found, if possible.

___ 5. If the treatments were administered by people other than the researcher, were these people properly trained?

Comment: Researchers often rely on other people such as graduate assistants, teachers, and psychologists to administer the treatments they are examining in an experiment. When this is the case, it is desirable for the researcher to assure the readers that they were properly trained. Otherwise, it is possible that the treatments were modified in some unknown way. Example 9.5.1 shows a statement regarding the training of three assistants who administered three types of training (the treatments). Hence, *training the trainers* refers to training those conducting the experimental training. Note that such statements are typically brief.

Example 9.5.1[4]

Excerpt on training those who administered the treatments:

Training the trainers. Scripts of the training sessions for the three conditions (recall, skills, and counseling education) were developed and critiqued by all four authors. The three trainers then met and practiced until they felt comfortable with the content of each session and assured that they could conduct each session effectively and consistently.

___ 6. If the treatments were administered by people other than the researcher, was there a check to see if they administered the treatments properly?

Comment: Even if those who administered the treatments were trained, they normally should be monitored. This is especially true for long and complex treatment cycles. For instance, if psychologists will be trying out new techniques with clients over a period of several months, it would be desirable to spot-check their efforts to determine whether they are applying their training properly. This can be done by directly observing them or by questioning them.

___ 7. If each treatment group had a different person administering a treatment, has the researcher tried to eliminate the "personal effect"?

Comment: Suppose that the purpose of an experiment is to compare the effectiveness of three methods for teaching decoding skills in first-grade reading instruction. If each method is used by a different teacher, differences in the teachers (such as ability to build rapport with students, level of enthusiasm, ability to build effective relationships with parents) may cause any observed differences in achievement (i.e, they may have had a "personal effect" on the outcome). One solution to this problem is to have each of the three methods used by a large number of teachers, with the teachers assigned at random to the methods. If such a large-scale study is not possible, another solution is to have each teacher use all three methods. In other words, Teacher A could use Methods X, Y, and Z at different points in time with different children; the

---

[4] Rochlen, A. B., Ligiero, D. P., Hill, C. E., & Heaton, K. J. (1999). Effects of training in dream recall and dream interpretation skills on dream recall, attitudes, and dream interpretation outcome. *Journal of Counseling Psychology, 46,* 27–34.

other two teachers would do likewise. When the results are averaged, each teacher will have contributed to the scores earned under each of the three methods.

___ 8. Except for differences in the treatments, were all other conditions the same in the experimental and control groups?

Comment: The results of an experiment can be influenced by many variables other than the independent variable. For example, if experimental and control groups are treated at different times of the day or in different rooms in a building (where one room is noisy and the other is not), these factors might influence the outcome of an experiment. We say that variables such as these are *confounding variables* because they confound the interpretation.

Many researchers are silent on whether all other conditions were controlled by making them the same for all groups in an experiment. Undoubtedly, many of them believe that readers will assume that the researcher is aware of this requirement for a good experiment and has met it without having to discuss it. In other cases, you may have some legitimate concerns about this issue. For example, if a researcher tells you that the experimental treatment was administered to children in one teacher's class while the children in another teacher's class served as controls, you may have concerns about the comparability of the two teachers' classrooms.

___ 9. If necessary, did the researchers disguise the purpose of the experiment from the participants?

Comment: If participants know the true, exact purpose of an experiment, their responses may be influenced by this knowledge. For example, in a study on the effects of a film showing negative consequences of drinking alcohol, the experimental group participants might report more negative attitudes toward alcohol simply because they know the researcher has hypothesized that this will happen. In other words, sometimes participants try to give researchers what they think the researchers expect. This is known as a *demand characteristic*. It is called this because it is as though a researcher is subtly demanding a certain outcome.

Certain types of instruments are more prone to the effects of demand characteristics than others. Self-report measures (such as self-reported attitudes toward alcohol) are especially sensitive to them. On the other hand, an achievement test is less sensitive because a student who does not have the skills being tested will not be successful on the test even if he or she is trying to please the researcher. Likewise, many physical measures are insensitive to this type of influence. In an experiment on methods for reducing HIV, for example, a subject will not be able to alter the results of a blood test for HIV.

Example 9.9.1 shows how a researcher attempted to blunt knowledge of the expected experimental outcome.

Example 9.9.1[5]

Excerpt on disguising the purpose of an experiment:

After watching the film, participants were asked to fill out a questionnaire containing questions for measuring alcohol-related attitudes, preceded by some unrelated items that were intended to keep them from getting to know the research purpose.

In Example 9.9.2, the experimenter wanted to measure attitudes toward residents of Newfoundland (a province in Canada whose residents are sometimes made fun of by other Canadians). It seemed better to disguise this true purpose by indicating that it was a study of perceptions people have of Canadians from all provinces and make it seem as though each participant just happened to draw Newfoundland as a province to which to react.

Example 9.9.2[6]

Excerpt on disguising the purpose of an experiment:

They [the participants] were told that because of time constraints, it would not be possible to ask each participant about every province. Consequently, each participant was asked to randomly draw a province from a cup. (All slips in the cup were labeled "Newfoundland.")

Although it is sometimes desirable to deceive participants (at least temporarily) for methodological reasons, this can raise ethical issues that a researcher would want to consider carefully. Most colleges and universities have review boards that can provide input on this matter.

____ 10. Is the setting for the experiment "natural"?

Comment: Sometimes researchers conduct experiments in unnatural settings. When they do this, they limit their study's *external validity*, that is, what is

---

[5] Bahk, C. M. (1997). The impact of presence versus absence of negative consequences in dramatic portrayals of alcohol drinking. *Journal of Alcohol and Drug Education, 42,* 18–26.
[6] Maio, G. R., Olson, J. M., & Bush, J. (1997). Telling jokes that disparage social groups: Effects on the joke teller's stereotypes. *Journal of Applied Social Psychology, 27,* 1986–2000.

found in the unnatural environment of a study may not be found in more natural settings (i.e., the finding may not be valid in a more natural setting).

Experiments conducted in laboratory settings often have poor external validity. Notice the unnatural aspects of Example 9.10.1. First, the amount and type of alcoholic beverages were assigned. Second, the female was a cohort of the experimenter (not someone the males were actually dating). Third, the setting was a laboratory, where the males would be likely to suspect that their behavior was being monitored in some way. While the researchers have achieved a high degree of control over the experiment, they have sacrificed external validity in the process.

Example 9.10.1
Experiment with poor external validity:

A research team was interested in the effects of alcohol consumption on aggressiveness in males when dating. In their experiment, some of the males were given moderate amounts of beer to consume. Then all males were observed interacting with a female cohort of the experimenters. The interactions took place in a laboratory on a college campus, and observations were made through a one-way mirror.

___ 11. Has the researcher used politically acceptable and ethical treatments?

Comment: This evaluation question is applicable primarily to experiments in applied areas such as education, clinical psychology, social work, and medicine. For example, has the researcher used treatments to promote classroom discipline that will be acceptable to parents, teachers, and the community? Or, has the researcher used methods such as moderate corporal punishment by teachers, which will probably be unacceptable to many people?

A low mark on this question means that the experiment is unlikely to have an impact in the applied area in which it was conducted.

___ 12. Has the researcher distinguished between *random selection* and *random assignment*?

Comment: The desirability of using *random selection* to obtain samples from which we can generalize with confidence to larger populations was discussed in Chapter 6. Such selection is highly desirable in any study—whether it is an experiment or not. *Random assignment*, on the other hand, refers to the process for assigning participants to the various treatment conditions (i.e., to the treatments, including any control condition).

Note that in any given experiment, *selection* may or may not be random. Likewise, *assignment* may or may not be random. Figure 9.12.1 illustrates the ideal situation where first there is random selection from a population of interest to obtain a sample. This is followed by random assignment of individuals to treatment conditions.

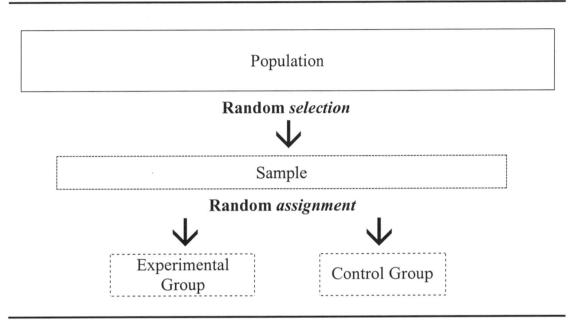

Figure 9.12.1.   Ideal combination of random selection and random assignment

When discussing the generalizability of the results of an experiment, a researcher should do so in light of the type of *selection* used. On the other hand, when discussing the comparability of the two groups, he or she should consider the type of *assignment* used.

___ 13. Overall, was the experiment properly conducted?

Comment: Rate the overall quality of the experimental procedures based on the answers to the evaluation questions in this chapter and any other concerns you may have.

Concluding Comment

This chapter presents a common-sense approach to the evaluation of experiments. For those of you who are using this book in coordination with a traditional research methods textbook, a few comments on terminology are in order. First, most such textbooks distinguish between *internal validity* and *external validity*. We say that an experiment has high *internal validity* when the differences in treatment are the only logical possible cause for any observed differences among groups. Evaluation Questions 1 through 8 in this chapter deal with this issue. On the other hand, we say that an experiment has high *external validity* when we can have confidence that the results apply to the population to which the researcher wishes to generalize. Evaluation Questions 9 through 11 deal with this second issue. Evaluation Question 12 deals with both these issues because *random selection* contributes to a study's external validity while *random assignment* contributes to its internal validity.

As a final matter, an experiment to which participants are assigned at random is said to be a *true experiment*. An experiment in which groups are formed in a nonrandom fashion but on which we have data suggesting that they are initially equal is said to be a *quasi-experiment*.[7] Experiments of lesser quality (such as not having a control condition or comparing two groups that are not formed at random and for which we have no data on their initial equality) are said to be *pre-experiments*.

Exercise for Chapter 9

Directions: Locate several experiments on topics of interest to you in academic journals. Evaluate them in light of the evaluation questions in this chapter as well as any other considerations and concerns you may have. Select the one to which you gave the highest overall rating and bring it to class for discussion. Be prepared to discuss both its strengths and weaknesses.

---

[7] Quasi-experimental designs include single-subject/behavior analysis designs that have reversals (see Evaluation Question 3). These are not true designs, by definition, because they do not include random assignment of individuals to groups.

Chapter 10

Evaluating Results Sections

In quantitative reports, the results section almost always contains statistics that summarize the data that were collected and describes the results of significance testing. In qualitative reports, the results section consists of a description of themes and trends, frequently supplemented with quotations (often called "verbatims") from participants.

In this chapter, it is assumed that you have basic knowledge of elementary statistical methods.

___ 1. Is the results section a cohesive essay?

Comment: The results section should be an essay—not just a collection of statistics or quotations from participants. In other words, researchers should describe results in paragraphs, each of which describes some aspect of the results. These paragraphs usually will contain statistics (when a study is quantitative), but the gist of the results should be clear even if one ignores the statistics. This is illustrated in Example 10.1.1, where the words describe the major results, which are supported by statistics. Also notice the use of the transitional term "however," which signals this anomaly in the results: While the non-Asians were more confident, they scored lower. The researchers, quite correctly, are guiding their readers through the results—not just letting the statistics speak for themselves.

Example 10.1.1[1]
Main ideas expressed in words, supported by statistics:

Regarding self-efficacy beliefs, non-Asian students appeared more confident with their abilities to accomplish the verbal tasks by reporting higher levels of self-efficacy beliefs ($M = 3.02$ out of 4; $SD = .67$), t (287.28) = 2.25, = $p < .05$. However, Asian American students out-performed their non-Asian counterparts by scoring approximately 90% on the achievement assessment, whereas the non-Asian students scored approximately 75%.

---

[1] Eaton, M. J. & Dembo, M. H. (1997). Differences in the motivational beliefs of Asian American and non-Asian students. *Journal of Educational Psychology*, *89*, 433-440.

___ 2. Does the researcher refer back to the research hypotheses, purposes, or questions originally stated in the introduction?

Comment: This evaluation question may not be applicable to a very short research report with a single hypothesis, question, or purpose. When there are several of these, however, readers should be shown how different elements of the results relate to the specific hypotheses, questions, or purposes, as illustrated in Example 10.2.1. The authors of this example had only two hypotheses and refer to them by their ordinal position ("first" and "second"). When there are more, it is helpful if the authors recap or restate them in the results section.

Example 10.2.1[2]
Referring to specific hypotheses in a results section:

Supporting the first hypothesis, chi-square analysis showed that the two groups were proportionately different on self-reported changes in frequency of exercise (Table 2) and intensity of exercise (Table 3). The experimental group on both measures showed greater changes than the control group. Twenty-five percent.... [Note that the tables referred to here are not shown in this book.]

In support of the second hypothesis, Pearson *r* indicated a statistically significant association between scores on....

___ 3. When there are a number of statistics, have they been presented in table form?

Comment: Even when there are as few as six statistics, a table can be helpful. For example, if three groups are being compared, and there is a mean (the most common average) and standard deviation for each, a paragraph in which all of these statistics are embedded could be hard to follow. On the other hand, a table in which all of the means are in the same row or column enables a reader to quickly scan and compare them.

___ 4. If there are tables, are their important aspects discussed in the narrative of the results section?

Comment: Researchers should point out the important highlights of their statistical tables, as illustrated in Example 10.4.1.

---

[2] Huddy, D. C., Hebert, J. L., Hyner, G. C., & Johnson, R. L. (1995). Facilitating changes in exercise behavior: Effect of structured statements of intention on perceived barriers to action. *Psychological Reports, 76*, 867–875.

Example 10.4.1[3]

A table with highlights discussed:

Total responses for time spent in recreational reading each week while classes are in session are shown in Table 1. While classes are in session, 63% of the respondents report reading 2 hours or less each week. At the other end of the continuum, only 13% of students surveyed report 6 or more hours per week when classes are in session.

Table 1   *Time spent reading recreationally: Classes in session*

Hours per week	Number of students	Percentage of students
Less than 1 hour	40	29
1-2 hours	47	34
3-5 hours	33	24
6-10 hours	12	8
More than 10 hours	7	5

___ 5. Have the researchers presented descriptive statistics before presenting the results of inferential tests?

Comment: Descriptive statistics include frequencies, percentages, averages (usually the mean or median), measures of variability (usually the standard deviation or interquartile range). In addition, correlation coefficients (usually the Pearson *r*) describe the direction and strength of relationships.

Inferential statistics determine the probability that any differences among descriptive statistics are due to chance (random sampling error). Obviously, it makes no sense to discuss the results of a test on descriptive statistics unless the descriptive statistics have first been presented. Failure on this evaluation question is very rare.

___ 6. If any differences are statistically significant and small, have the researchers noted that they are small?

Comment: For technical reasons that are beyond the scope of this book, statistically significant differences are sometimes very small. When this is the case, it is a good idea for a researcher to point this out. Obviously, a very small but statistically significant difference will be interpreted differently from a large

---

[3] Gallik, J. D. (1999). Do they read for pleasure? Recreational reading habits of college students. *Journal of Adolescent & Adult Literacy, 42*, 480-488.

and statistically significant difference. Example 10.6.1 illustrates how this might be pointed out.[4]

> **Example 10.6.1**
> *Description of a small but statistically significant difference:*
>
> Although the difference between the means of the experimental (M = 24.55) and control group (M = 23.65) was statistically significant (t = 2.075, p < .05), the small size of the difference, in absolute terms, suggests that the effects of the experimental treatment were weak.

This evaluation question is posed because researchers sometimes incorrectly believe that simply because a difference is statistically significant, it must be large enough to be important. They fail to understand that a significant difference is merely one that is unlikely to have been produced by chance. Note that there are no mathematical formulas (or tests) to determine the practical importance of a difference.

___ 7. Have appropriate statistics been selected?

Comment: This is often a difficult question to answer because readers of reports typically do not have access to the original data so they are unable to check for characteristics such as skewedness (if a distribution is highly skewed the median should be preferred over the mean) or linearity (if the relationship between two variables is not linear, the Pearson r is inappropriate). This problem is compounded by the fact that very few researchers discuss whether they checked for such characteristics of their data before selecting statistics. Nevertheless, this evaluation question is posed because you may occasionally be able to spot the inappropriate selection of statistics.

___ 8. Overall, is the presentation of the results adequate?

Comment: Rate this evaluation question after considering your answers to the earlier ones in this chapter and any additional considerations and concerns you may have.

---

[4] An increasingly popular statistic, *effect size*, is designed to draw readers' attention to the size of any significant difference. In general terms, it indicates by how many standard deviations two groups differ from each other. Unfortunately, its use is not very widespread to date.

Exercise for Chapter 10

Directions: Locate several research reports of interest to you in academic journals. Read them and evaluate the descriptions of the results in light of the evaluation questions in this chapter as well as any other considerations and concerns you may have. Select the one to which you gave the highest overall rating and bring it to class for discussion. Be prepared to discuss both its strengths and weaknesses.

Notes:

Chapter 11

Evaluating Discussion Sections

The last section of a report typically has the heading "Discussion." However, expect to see some variations such as "Discussion and Conclusions" or "Conclusions and Implications."

___ **1. In long articles, do the researchers briefly summarize the purpose and results at the beginning of the discussion?**

Comment: A brief summary at this point in a long article helps keep readers focused on the big picture.

___ **2. Do the researchers acknowledge their methodological limitations?**

Comment: Although the methodological limitations and weaknesses may be discussed at any point in a research report, they are frequently included in the discussion section because any conclusions should be drawn in light of the limitations. These are often discussed under the subheading "Limitations." Examples 11.2.1 and 11.2.2 show portions of such discussions.

Example 11.2.1[1]
Acknowledgment of a limitation in a discussion section:

As with all research studies, certain limitations of the study must be acknowledged when the implications of study results are considered. The correlational design of this study precludes the assumption of a causal relationship.... The generalizability of the results is somewhat limited by the sampling procedures. It is possible that those participants who returned the research materials differed in some significant way from those who did not....

---

[1] McCracken, R. S. & Weitzman, L. M. (1997). Relationship of personal agency, problem-solving appraisal, and traditionality of career choice to women's attitudes toward multiple role planning. *Journal of Counseling Psychology, 44,* 149–159.

Example 11.2.2[2]

Acknowledgment of a limitation in a discussion section:

This study surveyed men and women who, at the time of participation, were college juniors and seniors. Some sections of the survey instrument asked participants to respond with respect to their early experiences in science and engineering majors. For some of the scales, this required retrospective responses that may have been difficult for the participants and that may have been contaminated by more recent experiences.

___ **3. Are the results discussed in terms of the literature cited in the introduction?**

Comment: The literature cited in the introduction sets the stage for the report. It makes sense to finish the report with at least a passing mention of how the current study "fits" into the larger body of literature. Are the results consistent with those in the literature? With only some of them? With none of them? These are important issues to consider when drawing conclusions from a particular study. Examples 11.3.1 and 11.3.2 illustrate how some researchers address this issue.

Example 11.3.1[3]

Discussion in terms of literature mentioned in the introduction:

Our work agreed with past studies suggesting that constructivist approaches to working with teachers help them develop the deeper knowledge that is needed so they can teach in newer, more intellectually challenging ways (Cohen & Spillane, 1993).

Example 11.3.2[4]

Discussion in terms of literature mentioned in the introduction:

Why might our results differ so markedly from those of Lee and Bryk (1986) and others? One possibility is that something important about Catholic schools has changed since 1980.... Throughout the 1980s and early 1990s, a significant number of Catholic secondary schools...closed their doors while many other single-sex Catholic schools merged....

---

[2] Schaefers, K. G., Epperson, D. L., & Nauta, M. M. (1997). Women's career development: Can theoretically derived variables predict persistence in engineering majors? *Journal of Counseling Psychology, 44,* 173–183.

[3] Firestone, W. A. & Pennell, J. R. (1997). Designing state-sponsored teacher networks: A comparison of two cases. *American Educational Research Journal, 34,* 237–266.

[4] LePore, P. C. & Warren, J. R. (1997). A comparison of single-sex and coeducational Catholic secondary schooling: Evidence from the National Educational Longitudinal Study of 1988. *American Educational Research Journal, 34,* 485–511.

___ 4. Have the researchers avoided citing new references in the discussion?

Comment: The relevant literature should be first cited in the introduction. This is akin to laying all the cards on the table. The literature referred to in the discussion section should be limited to that originally cited in the introduction.

___ 5. Are specific implications discussed?

Comment: Applied research usually has implications for practicing professionals. To be helpful, a statement of implications should state specifically what a person, group, or institution should do if the results of the study are correct. This is illustrated in Example 11.5.1.

Example 11.5.1[5]
A statement of specific implications in a study on advice given to parents on sexuality in the popular press:

The popular press also needs to be more sensitive to different cultures and contemporary family forms. Only a few of the articles surveyed mentioned cultural differences in discussions about sexuality…. Since the majority [of families] are either single-parent or blended families, it may be helpful for authors to provide information on how to approach the topic of sexuality from the perspective of stepparents or single parents living with a child of the opposite sex.

Likewise, theoretical research has implications for those who are building and refining theories.

___ 6. Are suggestions for future research specific?

Comment: It is uninformative for researchers to conclude with a simple phrase such as "more research is needed." To be helpful, researchers should point to specific procedures and methods that might be fruitful in future research. This is illustrated in Example 11.6.1.

---

[5] Simanski, J. W. (1998). The birds and the bees: An analysis of advice given to parents through the popular press. *Adolescence, 33,* 33-45.

Example 11.6.1[6]
Specific suggestion for future research:

Perhaps future research could assess the function of self-presentation in therapy more directly. For example, clients could be asked questions at intake concerning what impression they would like to make on their counselors and how they expect to be seen and would like to be seen by the counselors. After therapy is under way, they could be asked....

___ **7. Have the researchers distinguished between speculation and data-based conclusions?**

Comment: It is perfectly acceptable for researchers to speculate in the discussion section (e.g., what the results might have been if the methodology had been different). However, it is important that researchers clearly distinguish between their speculation and the conclusions that can be justified by the data they have gathered.

___ **8. Overall, is the discussion effective and appropriate?**

Comment: Rate this evaluation question after considering your answers to the earlier ones in this chapter and any additional considerations and concerns you may have.

Exercise for Chapter 11

Directions: Locate several research reports of interest to you in academic journals. Read them and evaluate the discussion sections in light of the evaluation questions in this chapter as well as any other considerations and concerns you may have. Select the one to which you gave the highest overall rating and bring it to class for discussion. Be prepared to discuss both its strengths and weaknesses.

---

[6] Kelly, A. E. (1998). Client's secret keeping in outpatient therapy. *Journal of Counseling Psychology, 45,* 50–57.

Chapter 12

Putting It All Together

If you have been faithfully applying the evaluation questions in Chapters 2 through 11, you have a series of "yes/no" answers and ratings from 1 to 5. Now it is time to put it all together and arrive at an overall evaluation. This should not be done in some mechanical manner such as summing the number of times you answered "yes." Instead, you should make some overall judgments by looking at the big picture and considering the realities of conducting research in the social and behavioral sciences. The following evaluation questions are designed to help you do this.

____ 1. Have the researchers selected an important problem?

Comment: In Chapter 4, you were asked to consider whether the researchers established the importance of their problem. The evaluation question we are considering here is somewhat different from the one in Chapter 4 because this one asks whether, in your judgment, the problem is important—even if the researchers have failed to make a strong case for it. This judgment needs to be made because a methodologically strong study on a trivial problem is doomed from the beginning. On the other hand, a weak study on an important topic may make a contribution to a field of study—especially if there are no stronger studies available on the same topic.

____ 2. Were the researchers reflective?

Comment: Researchers should reflect on their methodological decisions and share these reflections with their readers. This shows that careful thinking underlies their work. For example, do they reflect on why they worked with one kind of sample rather than another? Do they discuss their reasons for selecting one instrument over another for use in their research? Do they discuss their rationale for other design and procedural decisions they made in designing and conducting their research?

Researchers should also reflect on their interpretations of the data. Are there other ways to interpret it? Are the various possible interpretations described and evaluated? Do they make it clear why they favor one interpretation over another?

___ 3. Is the report cohesive?

Comment: Do the researchers make clear the heart of the matter (usually the research hypotheses, purposes, or questions) and write a report that revolves around it and is cohesive (that is, flows logically from one section to another)? Note that a scattered, incoherent report has little chance of making an important contribution.

___ 4. Does the report extend the boundaries of our knowledge on a topic?

Comment: By introducing new variables or improved methods, researchers are often able to expand our understanding of a problem. When they do this, researchers usually comment on it, as illustrated in Example 12.4.1.

> ### Example 12.4.1[1]
> *Researchers describe improvements that will help expand understanding of a topic:*
>
> The present research builds on previous research on lying in relationships in several important ways. First, it is more comprehensive than previous studies in which participants selected just one particular lie (Hample, 1980) or conversation (Turner et al., 1975) or situation (Metts, 1989) to describe. Second, it is the only research to include a measure of participants' opportunities to lie, that is, the number of social interactions they had with each partner.... Third, the community member sample described in this report…is the only group we know of in the literature on lying in everyday life that is not a group consisting solely of college students. Finally, the present research is especially comprehensive in the number of ways that relationships are assessed. Relationship type was documented, and patterns of lying were compared across the different types.

___ 5. Are any major methodological flaws unavoidable or forgivable?

Comment: No study is perfect, but some are more seriously flawed than others. When serious flaws are encountered, consider whether they were unavoidable. For example, getting a random sample of street prostitutes for a study on AIDS transmission is probably impossible. However, if the researchers went to the

---

[1] DePaulo, B. M. & Kashy, D. A. (1998). Everyday lies in close and casual relationships. *Journal of Personality and Social Psychology, 74*, 63-79.

trouble to contact them at different times of the day in various locations (not just the safer parts of a city) and obtained a high rate of participation from those who were contacted, the failure to obtain a random sample would be forgivable because the flaw was unavoidable. Contrast this with researchers who want to generalize from a sample of fourth graders to a larger population but simply settle for a classroom of students who are readily accessible because they attend the university's demonstration school on the university campus. The failure to use random sampling or at least get a more diverse sample is not unavoidable and should be counted as a serious flaw.

Likewise, flaws in measurement (such as the unavailability of a highly valid instrument) or experimental design (such as the inability to assign at random for institutional or ethical reasons) may be forgivable.

Unless we tolerate some flaws under some circumstances, the vast majority of research in the social and behavioral sciences would need to be summarily rejected. Instead, as a practical matter, we tolerate certain flaws but interpret the data from seriously flawed studies with considerable caution.

____ 6. Is the research likely to inspire additional research?

Comment: Strong arguments for the importance of taking a closer look at a previously understudied problem, unique or improved methods that overcome flaws in previous studies, and interesting results that have practical and theoretical implications are likely to inspire additional research.

Even if a study is seriously flawed, its publication can be justified if it inspires others to study the problem—especially if they study it in different ways, with different samples, and, most important, with fewer major flaws. Keep in mind that research on a problem is an ongoing *process*, with each study contributing to our knowledge base. A study that stimulates the process and moves it forward is worthy of our attention—even if it is seriously flawed or is only a pilot study.

____ 7. Is the research likely to help in decision-making (either of a practical or theoretical nature)?

Comment: Even seriously flawed research sometimes can help decision-makers. Suppose a researcher conducted an experiment on a new drug-resistance educational program with no control group (usually considered a serious flaw) and found that students' illicit drug usage actually went up from pretest to posttest. Such a finding might lead the programs' funding agency to proceed cautiously before refunding or expanding the program, especially if other studies with different types of flaws produced results consistent with this one.

When applying this evaluation question, ask yourself how comfortable you would be making an important decision based on a study you are evaluating. In the absence of any other studies on the same topic, would this study help you make a more informed decision than if the study did not exist?

___ **8. All things considered, is the report worthy of publication in an academic journal?**

Comment: Given that space is limited in academic journals, with some journals rejecting more than 90% of the research reports submitted, is the report you are evaluating worthy of publication?

___ **9. Would you be proud to have your name on the report as a co-author?**

Comment: Arguably, this is the most subjective evaluation question in this book, and it is fitting that it is last. Would you want to be associated with the research you are evaluating?

Concluding Comment

I hope that as a result of reading and working through this book, you have become a critical consumer of research while recognizing that conducting solid research is difficult and, at times, impossible. The typical research methods textbook attempts to show *what should be done in the ideal*. This is understandable because the usual purpose of such books is to train students in how to conduct research. Unless a student knows what the ideal is, he or she is likely to fall unintentionally into many traps. However, when evaluating reports of research in academic journals, it is unreasonable to hold each article up to ideal standards. Researchers conduct research under less-than-ideal conditions, usually with limited resources. In addition, they are forced to make compromises given the practical realities of their research settings. A fair and meaningful evaluation takes these matters into consideration.

Appendix A[1]

Quantitative and Qualitative Research: An Overview

Because *quantitative* researchers reduce information to statistics such as averages, percentages, and so on, their research reports are easy to spot. If a report has a results section devoted mainly to the presentation of statistical data, it is a safe bet that it is a report of quantitative research. This approach to research has dominated the social and behavioral sciences throughout the 1900s, so for most topics, you are likely to locate many more articles reporting quantitative research than qualitative research.

The literature on how to conduct quantitative research *emphasizes*:

1. Starting with one or more very specific, explicitly stated research hypotheses, purposes, or questions, ideally derived from theory and/or previous research. Research plans focus narrowly on the stated hypotheses, purposes, or questions (as opposed to being wide ranging).
2. Selecting a random sample (like drawing names out of a hat) from a particular population so that the sample is representative of the population from which it was drawn.[2]
3. Using a relatively large sample of participants, sometimes as many as 1,500 for a national survey. Some quantitative researchers use even larger samples, but many use much smaller ones due to limited resources. A study with a large sample is usually a quantitative one. However, a study with a small sample could be either quantitative or qualitative.
4. Making observations with instruments that can be scored objectively such as multiple-choice achievement tests and attitude scales in response to which participants mark choices such as "strongly agree" to "strongly disagree."
5. Presenting results using statistics and making inferences to the population from which the sample was drawn (i.e., inferring that what the researcher found by studying a sample is similar to what he or she would have found by studying the entire population from which the sample was drawn).

---

[1] This appendix is based in part on material drawn with permission from Galvan, J. L. (1999). *Writing Literature Reviews: A Guide for Students of the Social and Behavioral Sciences.* Los Angeles: Pyrczak Publishing.

[2] It is "representative" except for the effects of random errors, which can be assessed with inferential statistics. Chapter 7 points out that researchers do not always sample or need random samples.

In addition, quantitative research is characterized by "distance" between researchers and their subjects (i.e., participants). That is, quantitative researchers typically have limited contact with their subjects. In fact, it is not uncommon for the researcher to have no direct contact. For example, a quantitative researcher might have teachers administer tests to students without ever seeing or talking with the students. Even if the researcher is physically present in the research setting, he or she usually sticks to a script for the study and avoids unplanned personal interactions.

Qualitative research also has a long tradition in the social and behavioral sciences, but has gained a large following in many applied fields only in recent decades. It is also easy to spot, first, because the titles of the articles will often contain the word "qualitative." In addition, qualitative researchers usually identify their research as qualitative in their introductions as well as in other parts of their reports.[3] You can also spot it because the results sections will be presented in terms of a narrative describing themes and trends—very often illustrated with quotations from the participants.

The literature on how to conduct qualitative research *emphasizes*:

1. Starting with a general research question or problem, and *not* formulating hypotheses derived from previously published literature or theories. Although qualitative researchers avoid starting with hypotheses, they may emerge (i.e., a researcher may formulate hypotheses that explain his or her observations) while conducting the research. Such hypotheses are subject to change as additional data are collected during the study. Thus, there is a fluid interaction between the data and any hypotheses.

2. Selecting a purposive sample—not a random one. A purposive sample is one in which the researcher has some special research interest and is not necessarily representative of a larger population. In other words, the researcher intentionally draws what he or she believes to be an appropriate sample for the research problem. For example, for a study of career development of highly achieving women, one group of researchers recently selected women who were identified in the media and by professional organizations as being leaders.[4] Thus, they were purposively identified—*not* selected at random.

3. Using a relatively small sample—sometimes as small as one exemplary case, but more often small groups of people or units such as classrooms, churches, and so on.

4. Observing with relatively unstructured instruments such as semistructured interviews, unstructured direct observations, and so on.

---

[3] Note that quantitative researchers rarely explicitly state that their research is quantitative. Because the overwhelming majority of research reports in journals is quantitative, readers will assume that it is quantitative unless told otherwise.

[4] Richie, B. S. et al. (1997). Persistence, connection, and passion: A qualitative study of the career development of highly achieving African American–Black and White women. *Journal of Counseling Psychology, 44,* 133–148.

5. Observing intensively (e.g., spending extended periods of time with the participants to gain in-depth insights into the phenomena of interest).
6. Presenting results mainly or exclusively in words with an emphasis on understanding the particular purposive sample studied and usually de-emphasizing generalizations to larger populations.

In addition, qualitative research is characterized by the researchers' awareness of their own orientations, biases, and experiences that might affect their collection and interpretation of data. It is not uncommon for qualitative researchers to include in their research reports a statement on these issues and what steps they took to get beyond their own subjective experiences to understand their research problems from the participants' points of view. Thus, there is a tendency for qualitative research to be personal and interactive. This is in contrast to quantitative research in which researchers attempt to be objective and distant.

As you can see from the above, the fact that the two research traditions are quite distinct will need to be taken into account when evaluating research reports. Because quantitative research is still by far the dominant type in academic journals, this book emphasizes its evaluation, with comments throughout when evaluation criteria may need to be modified for the evaluation of qualitative research. Those of you who are just beginning to learn about qualitative research are urged to read Appendix B in this book, which discusses some important issues in its evaluation.

Notes:

Examining the Validity Structure of Qualitative Research

R. BURKE JOHNSON
University of South Alabama

ABSTRACT. Three types of validity in qualitative research are discussed. First, descriptive validity refers to the factual accuracy of the account as reported by the qualitative researcher. Second, interpretive validity is obtained to the degree that the participants' viewpoints, thoughts, intentions, and experiences are accurately understood and reported by the qualitative researcher. Third, theoretical validity is obtained to the degree that a theory or theoretical explanation developed from a research study fits the data and is, therefore, credible and defensible. The two types of validity that are typical of quantitative research, internal and external validity, are also discussed for qualitative research. Twelve strategies used to promote research validity in qualitative research are discussed.

From *Education*, *118*, 282–292. Copyright © 1997 by Project Innovation. Reprinted with permission of the publisher and author.

Discussions of the term "validity" have traditionally been attached to the quantitative research tradition. Not surprisingly, reactions by qualitative researchers have been mixed regarding whether or not this concept
5 should be applied to qualitative research. At the extreme, some qualitative researchers have suggested that the traditional quantitative criteria of reliability and validity are not relevant to qualitative research (e.g., Smith, 1984). Smith contends that the basic epistemo-
10 logical and ontological assumptions of quantitative and qualitative research are incompatible, and, therefore, the concepts of reliability and validity should be abandoned. Most qualitative researchers, however, probably hold a more moderate viewpoint. Most qualitative re-
15 searchers argue that some qualitative research studies are better than others, and they frequently use the term validity to refer to this difference. When qualitative researchers speak of research validity, they are usually referring to qualitative research that is plausible, credi-
20 ble, trustworthy, and, therefore, defensible. We believe it is important to think about the issue of validity in qualitative research and to examine some strategies that

have been developed to maximize validity (Kirk & Miller, 1986; LeCompte & Preissle, 1993; Lincoln &
25 Guba, 1985; Maxwell, 1996). A list of these strategies is provided in Table 1.

One potential threat to validity that researchers must be careful to watch out for is called *researcher bias.* This problem is summed up in a statement a col-
30 league of mine once made to me. She said, "The problem with qualitative research is that the researchers find what they want to find, and then they write up their results." It is true that the problem of researcher bias is frequently an issue because qualitative research
35 is open-ended and less structured than quantitative research. This is because qualitative research tends to be exploratory. (One would be remiss, however, to think that researcher bias is never a problem in quantitative research!) Researcher bias tends to result from selec-
40 tive observation and selective recording of information, and also from allowing one's personal views and perspectives to affect how data are interpreted and how the research is conducted.

The key strategy used to understand researcher bias
45 is called *reflexivity,* which means that the researcher actively engages in critical self-reflection about his or her potential biases and predispositions (Table 1). Through reflexivity, researchers become more self-aware, and they monitor and attempt to control their
50 biases. Many qualitative researchers include a distinct section in their research proposals titled Researcher Bias. In this section, they discuss their personal background, how it may affect their research, and what strategies they will use to address the potential prob-
55 lem. Another strategy that qualitative researchers use to reduce the effect of researcher bias is called *negative case sampling* (Table 1). This means that they attempt carefully and purposively to search for examples that disconfirm their expectations and explanations about
60 what they are studying. If you use this approach, you will find it more difficult to ignore important information, and you will come up with more credible and de-

Table 1
Strategies Used to Promote Qualitative Research Validity

Strategy	Description
Researcher as "Detective"	A metaphor characterizing the qualitative researcher as he or she searches for evidence about causes and effects. The researcher develops an understanding of the data through careful consideration of potential causes and effects and by systematically eliminating "rival" explanations or hypotheses until the final "case" is made "beyond a reasonable doubt." The "detective" can utilize any of the strategies listed here.
Extended fieldwork	When possible, qualitative researchers should collect data in the field over an extended period of time.
Low inference descriptors	The use of description phrased very close to the participants' accounts and researchers' field notes. Verbatims (i.e., direct quotations) are a commonly used type of low inference descriptors.
Triangulation	"Cross-checking" information and conclusions through the use of multiple procedures or sources. When the different procedures or sources are in agreement, you have "corroboration."
Data triangulation	The use of multiple data sources to help understand a phenomenon.
Methods triangulation	The use of multiple research methods to study a phenomenon.
Investigator triangulation	The use of multiple investigators (i.e., multiple researchers) in collecting and interpreting the data.
Theory triangulation	The use of multiple theories and perspectives to help interpret and explain the data.
Participant feedback	The feedback and discussion of the researcher's interpretations and conclusions with the actual participants and other members of the participant community for verification and insight.
Peer review	Discussion of the researcher's interpretations and conclusions with other people. This includes discussion with a "disinterested peer" (e.g., with another researcher not directly involved). This peer should be skeptical and play the "devil's advocate," challenging the researcher to provide solid evidence for any interpretations or conclusions. Discussion with peers who are familiar with the research can also help provide useful challenges and insights.
Negative case sampling	Locating and examining cases that disconfirm the researcher's expectations and tentative explanation.
Reflexivity	This involves self-awareness and "critical self-reflection" by the researcher on his or her potential biases and predispositions as these may affect the research process and conclusions.
Pattern matching	Predicting a series of results that form a "pattern" and then determining the degree to which the actual results fit the predicted pattern.

fensible results.

We will now examine some types of validity that
65 are important in qualitative research. We will start with
three types of validity that are especially relevant to
qualitative research (Maxwell, 1992, 1996). These
types are called descriptive validity, interpretive validity, and theoretical validity. They are important to
70 qualitative research because description of what is observed and interpretation of participants' thoughts are
two primary qualitative research activities. For example, ethnography produces descriptions and accounts of
the lives and experiences of groups of people with a
75 focus on cultural characteristics (Fetterman, 1998; LeCompte & Preissle, 1993). Ethnographers also attempt
to understand groups of people from the insider's perspective (i.e., from the viewpoints of the people in the
group; called the *emic* perspective). Developing a theo-
80 retical explanation of the behavior of group members is

also of interest to qualitative researchers, especially
qualitative researchers using the grounded theory perspective (Glaser & Strauss, 1967; Strauss and Corbin,
1990). After discussing these three forms of validity,
85 the traditional types of validity used in quantitative
research, internal and external validity, are discussed.
Internal validity is relevant when qualitative researchers explore cause and effect relationships. External
validity is relevant when qualitative researchers gener-
90 alize beyond their research studies.

Descriptive Validity

The first type of validity in qualitative research is
called *descriptive validity*. Descriptive validity refers to
the factual accuracy of the account as reported by the
researchers. The key questions addressed in descriptive
95 validity are: Did what was reported as taking place in
the group being studied actually happen? and Did the

researchers accurately report what they saw and heard? In other words, descriptive validity refers to accuracy in reporting descriptive information (e.g., description of events, objects, behaviors, people, settings, times, and places). This form of validity is important because description is a major objective in nearly all qualitative research.

One effective strategy used to obtain descriptive validity is called *investigator triangulation.* In the case of descriptive validity, investigator triangulation involves the use of multiple observers to record and describe the research participants' behavior and the context in which they were located. The use of multiple observers allows cross-checking of observations to make sure the investigators agree about what took place. When corroboration (i.e., agreement) of observations across multiple investigators is obtained, it is less likely that outside reviewers of the research will question whether something occurred. As a result, the research will be more credible and defensible.

Interpretive Validity

While descriptive validity refers to accuracy in reporting the facts, interpretive validity requires developing a window into the minds of the people being studied. *Interpretive validity* refers to accurately portraying the *meaning* attached by participants to what is being studied by the researcher. More specifically, it refers to the degree to which the research participants' viewpoints, thoughts, feelings, intentions, and experiences are accurately understood by the qualitative researcher and portrayed in the research report. An important part of qualitative research is understanding research participants' inner worlds (i.e., their phenomenological worlds), and interpretive validity refers to the degree of accuracy in presenting these inner worlds. Accurate interpretive validity requires that the researcher get inside the heads of the participants, look through the participants' eyes, and see and feel what they see and feel. In this way, the qualitative researcher can understand things from the participants' perspectives and provide a valid account of these perspectives.

Some strategies for achieving interpretive validity are provided in Table 1. *Participant feedback* is perhaps the most important strategy (Table 1). This strategy has also been called "member checking" (Lincoln & Guba, 1985). By sharing your interpretations of participants' viewpoints with the participants and other members of the group, you may clear up areas of miscommunication. Do the people being studied agree with what you have said about them? While this strategy is not perfect, because some participants may attempt to put on a good face, useful information is frequently obtained and inaccuracies are often identified.

When writing the research report, using many low inference descriptors is also helpful so that the reader can experience the participants' actual language, dialect, and personal meanings (Table 1). A verbatim is the lowest inference descriptor of all because the participants' exact words are provided in direct quotations. Here is an example of a verbatim from a high school dropout who was part of an ethnographic study of high school dropouts:

> I wouldn't do the work. I didn't like the teacher and I didn't like my mom and dad. So, even if I did my work, I wouldn't turn it in. I completed it. I just didn't want to turn it in. I was angry with my mom and dad because they were talking about moving out of state at the time (Okey & Cusick, 1995: p. 257).

This verbatim provides some description (i.e., what the participant did) but it also provides some information about the participant's interpretations and personal meanings (which is the topic of interpretive validity). The participant expresses his frustration and anger toward his parents and teacher, and shares with us what homework meant to him at the time and why he acted as he did. By reading verbatims like this one, readers of a report can experience for themselves the participants' perspectives. Again, getting into the minds of research participants is a common goal in qualitative research, and Maxwell calls our accuracy in portraying this inner content interpretive validity.

Theoretical Validity

The third type of validity in qualitative research is called *theoretical validity.* You have theoretical validity to the degree that a theoretical explanation developed from a research study fits the data and, therefore, is credible and defensible. Theory usually refers to discussions of *how* a phenomenon operates and *why* it operates as it does. Theory is usually more abstract and less concrete than description and interpretation. Theory development moves beyond just the facts and provides an explanation of the phenomenon. In the words of Joseph Maxwell (1992):

> ...one could label the student's throwing of the eraser as an act of resistance, and connect this act to the repressive behavior or values of the teacher, the social structure of the school, and class relationships in U.S. society. The identification of the throwing as resistance constitutes the application of a theoretical construct....the connection of this to other aspects of the participants, the school, or the community constitutes the postulation of theoretical relationships among these constructs (p. 291).

In the above example, the theoretical construct called "resistance" is used to explain the student's behavior. Maxwell points out that the construct of resistance may also be related to other theoretical constructs or variables. In fact, theories are often developed by relating theoretical constructs.

A strategy for promoting theoretical validity is *extended fieldwork* (Table 1). This means that you should spend a sufficient amount of time studying your research participants and their setting so that you can have confidence that the patterns of relationships you believe are operating are stable and so that you can understand why these relationships occur. As you spend more time in the field collecting data and generating and testing your inductive hypotheses, your theoretical explanation may become more detailed and intricate. You may also decide to use the strategy called *theory triangulation* (Table 1; Denzin, 1989). This means that you would examine how the phenomenon being studied would be explained by different theories. The various theories might provide you with insights and help you develop a more cogent explanation. In a related way, you might also use investigator triangulation and consider the ideas and explanations generated by additional researchers studying the research participants.

As you develop your theoretical explanation, you should make some predictions based on the theory and test the accuracy of those predictions. When doing this, you can use the *pattern matching* strategy (Table 1). In pattern matching, the strategy is to make several predictions at once; then, if all of the predictions occur as predicted (i.e., if the pattern is found), you have evidence supporting your explanation. As you develop your theoretical explanation, you should also use the negative case sampling strategy mentioned earlier (Table 1). That is, you must always search for cases or examples that do not fit your explanation so that you do not simply find the data that support your developing theory. As a general rule, your final explanation should accurately reflect the majority of the people in your research study. Another useful strategy for promoting theoretical validity is called *peer review* (Table 1). This means that you should try to spend some time discussing your explanation with your colleagues so that they can search for problems with it. Each problem must then be resolved. In some cases, you will find that you will need to go back to the field and collect additional data. Finally, when developing a theoretical explanation, you must also think about the issues of internal validity and external validity to which we now turn.

Internal Validity

Internal validity is the fourth type of validity in qualitative research of interest to us. Internal validity refers to the degree to which a researcher is justified in concluding that an observed relationship is causal (Cook and Campbell, 1979). Often, qualitative researchers are not interested in cause and effect relationships. Sometimes, however, qualitative researchers are interested in identifying potential causes and effects. In fact, qualitative research can be very helpful in describing how phenomena operate (i.e., studying process) and in developing and testing preliminary causal hypotheses and theories (Campbell, 1979; Johnson, 1994; LeCompte & Preissle, 1993; Strauss, 1995; 1994).

When qualitative researchers identify potential cause and effect relationships, they must think about many of the same issues that quantitative researchers must consider. They should also think about the strategies used for obtaining theoretical validity discussed earlier. The qualitative researcher takes on the role of the detective searching for the true cause(s) of a phenomenon, examining each possible clue, and attempting to rule out each rival explanation generated (see *researcher as detective* in Table 1). When trying to identify a causal relationship, the researcher makes mental comparisons. The comparison might be to a hypothetical control group. Although a control group is rarely used in qualitative research, the researcher can think about what would have happened if the causal factor had not occurred. The researcher can sometimes rely on his or her expert opinion, as well as published research studies when available, in deciding what would have happened. Furthermore, if the event is something that occurs again the researcher can determine if the causal factor precedes the outcome. In other words, when the causal factor occurs again, does the effect follow?

When a researcher believes that an observed relationship is causal, he or she must also attempt to make sure that the observed change in the dependent variable is due to the independent variable and not to something else (e.g., a confounding extraneous variable). The successful researcher will always make a list of rival explanations or rival hypotheses, which are possible or plausible reasons for the relationship other than the originally suspected cause. Be creative and think of as many rival explanations as you can. One way to get started is to be a skeptic and think of reasons why the relationship should not be causal. Each rival explanation must be examined after the list has been developed. Sometimes you will be able to check a rival explanation with the data you have already collected through additional data analysis. At other times you will need to collect additional data. One strategy would be to observe the relationship you believe to be causal under conditions where the confounding variable is not present and compare this outcome with the original outcome. For example, if you concluded that a teacher effectively maintained classroom discipline on a given day but a critic maintained that it was the result of a parent visiting the classroom on that day, then you should try to observe the teacher again when the parent is not present. If the teacher is still successful, you have some evidence that the original finding was not because of the presence of the parent in the classroom.

All of the strategies shown in Table 1 are used to improve the internal validity of qualitative research. Now we will explain the only two strategies not yet discussed (i.e., methods triangulation and data triangulation). When using *methods triangulation*, the researcher uses more than one method of research in a single research study. The word methods should be used broadly here, and it refers to different methods of research (e.g., ethnography, survey, experimental, etc.)

as well to different types of data collection procedures (e.g., interviews, questionnaires, and observations).
325 You can intermix any of these (e.g., ethnography and survey research methods, or interviews and observations, or experimental research and interviews). The logic is to combine different methods that have "nonoverlapping weaknesses and strengths" (Brewer &
330 Hunter, 1989). The weaknesses (and strengths) of one method will tend to be different from those of a different method, which means that when you combine two or more methods you will have better evidence! In other words, the "whole" is better than its "parts."

335   Here is an example of methods triangulation. Perhaps you are interested in why students in an elementary classroom stigmatize a certain student named Brian. A stigmatized student would be an individual that is not well liked, has a lower status, and is seen as
340 different from the normal students. Perhaps Brian has a different haircut from the other students, is dressed differently, or doesn't act like the other students. In this case, you might decide to observe how students treat Brian in various situations. In addition to observing the
345 students, you will probably decide to interview Brian and the other students to understand their beliefs and feelings about Brian. A strength of observational data is that you can actually see the students' behaviors. A weakness of interviews is that what the students say
350 and what they actually do may be different. However, using interviews you can delve into the students' thinking and reasoning, whereas you cannot do this using observational data. Therefore, the whole will likely be better than the parts.

355   When using *data triangulation*, the researcher uses multiple data sources in a single research study. "Data sources" does not mean using different methods. Data triangulation refers to the use of multiple data sources using a single method. For example, the use of multiple
360 interviews would provide multiple data sources while using a single method (i.e., the interview method). Likewise, the use of multiple observations would be another example of data triangulation; multiple data sources would be provided while using a single method
365 (i.e., the observational method). Another important part of data triangulation involves collecting data at different times, at different places, and with different people.

  Here is an example of data triangulation. Perhaps a researcher is interested in studying why certain stu-
370 dents are apathetic. It would make sense to get the perspectives of several different kinds of people. The researcher might interview teachers, interview students identified by the teachers as being apathetic, and interview peers of apathetic students. Then the researcher
375 could check to see if the information obtained from these different data sources was in agreement. Each data source may provide additional reasons as well as a different perspective on the question of student apathy, resulting in a more complete understanding of the phe-
380 nomenon. The researcher should also interview apa-

thetic students at different class periods during the day and in different types of classes (e.g., math and social studies). Through the rich information gathered (e.g., from different people, at different times, and at differ-
385 ent places) the researcher can develop a better understanding of why students are apathetic than if only one data source is used.

External Validity

  External validity is important when you want to generalize from a set of research findings to other peo-
390 ple, settings, and times (Cook and Campbell, 1979). Typically, generalizability is not the major purpose of qualitative research. There are at least two reasons for this. First, the people and settings examined in qualitative research are rarely randomly selected, and, as you
395 know, random selection is the best way to generalize from a sample to a population. As a result, qualitative research is virtually always weak in the form of population validity focused on "generalizing to populations" (i.e., generalizing from a sample to a population).

400   Second, some qualitative researchers are more interested in documenting particularistic findings than universalistic findings. In other words, in certain forms of qualitative research the goal is to show what is unique about a certain group of people, or a certain
405 event, rather than generate findings that are broadly applicable. At a fundamental level, many qualitative researchers do not believe in the presence of general laws or universal laws. General laws are things that apply to many people, and universal laws are things
410 that apply to everyone. As a result, qualitative research is frequently considered weak on the "generalizing across populations" form of population validity (i.e., generalizing to different kinds of people), and on ecological validity (i.e., generalizing across settings) and
415 temporal validity (i.e., generalizing across times).

  Other experts argue that rough generalizations can be made from qualitative research. Perhaps the most reasonable stance toward the issue of generalizing is that we can generalize to other people, settings, and
420 times to the degree that they are similar to the people, settings, and times in the original study. Stake (1990) uses the term *naturalistic generalization*[1] to refer to this process of generalizing based on similarity. The bottom line is this: The more similar the people and
425 circumstances in a particular research study are to the ones that you want to generalize to, the more defensible your generalization will be and the more readily you should make such a generalization.

  To help readers of a research report know when

---

[1] Donald Campbell (1986) makes a similar point, and he uses the term *proximal similarity* to refer to the degree of similarity between the people and circumstances in the original research study and the people and circumstances to which you wish to apply the findings. Using Campbell's term, your goal is to check for proximal similarity.

430 they can generalize, qualitative researchers should provide the following kinds of information: the number
and kinds of people in the study, how they were selected to be in the study, contextual information, the
nature of the researcher's relationship with the partici-
435 pants, information about any informants who provided
information, the methods of data collection used, and
the data analysis techniques used. This information is
usually reported in the Methodology section of the final research report. Using the information included in a
440 well-written methodology section, readers will be able
to make informed decisions about to whom the results
may be generalized. They will also have the information they will need if they decide to replicate the research study with new participants.

445   Some experts show another way to generalize from
qualitative research (e.g., Yin, 1994). Qualitative researchers can sometimes use *replication logic,* just like
the replication logic that is commonly used by experimental researchers when they generalize beyond the
450 people in their studies, even when they do not have
random samples. According to replication logic, the
more times a research finding is shown to be true with
different sets of people, the more confidence we can
place in the finding and in the conclusion that the
455 finding generalizes beyond the people in the original
research study (Cook and Campbell, 1979). In other
words, if the finding is replicated with different kinds
of people and in different places, then the evidence
may suggest that the finding applies very broadly.
460 Yin's key point is that there is no reason why replication logic cannot be applied to certain kinds of qualitative research.[2]

Here is an example. Over the years you may observe a certain pattern of relations between boys and
465 girls in your third-grade classroom. Now assume that
you decided to conduct a qualitative research study and
you find that the pattern of relation occurred in your
classroom and in two other third-grade classrooms you
studied. Because your research is interesting, you de-
470 cide to publish it. Then other researchers replicate your
study with other people and they find that the same
relationship holds in the third-grade classrooms they
studied. According to replication logic, the more times
a theory or a research finding is replicated with other
475 people, the greater the support for the theory or research finding. Now assume further that other researchers find that the relationship holds in classrooms
at several other grade levels (e.g., first grade, second
grade, fourth grade, and fifth grade). If this happens,
480 the evidence suggests that the finding generalizes to
students in other grade levels, adding additional gener-
ality to the finding.

---

[2] The late Donald Campbell, perhaps the most important
quantitative research methodologist over the past 50 years,
approved of Yin's (1994) book. See, for example, his introduction to that book.

We want to make one more comment before concluding. If generalizing through replication and theo-
485 retical validity (discussed above) sound similar, that is
because they are. Basically, generalizing (i.e., external
validity) is frequently part of theoretical validity. In
other words, when researchers develop theoretical explanations, they often want to generalize beyond their
490 original research study. Likewise, internal validity is
also important for theoretical validity if cause and effect statements are made.

References

Brewer, J., & Hunter, A. (1989). *Multimethod research: A synthesis of styles.* Newbury Park, CA: Sage.

Campbell, D.T. (1979). Degrees of freedom and the case study. In T.D. Cook & C.S. Reichardt (Eds.), *Qualitative and quantitative methods in evaluation research* (pp. 49–67). Beverly Hills, CA: Sage Publications.

Campbell, D.T. (1986). Relabeling internal and external validity for applied social scientists. In W. Trochim (Ed.), Advances in quasi-experimental design and analysis: *New Directions for Program Evaluation,* 31, San Francisco: Jossey-Bass.

Cook, T.D., & Campbell, D.T. (1979). *Quasi-experimentation: Design and analysis issues for field settings.* Chicago: Rand McNally.

Denzin, N.K. (1989). *The research act: Theoretical introduction to sociological methods.* Englewood Cliffs, NJ: Prentice Hall.

Fetterman, D.M. (1998). Ethnography. In *Handbook of Applied Social Research Methods* by L. Bickman & D.J. Rog (Eds.). Thousand Oaks, CA: Sage.

Glaser, B.G., & Strauss, A.L. (1967). *The discovery of grounded theory: Strategies for qualitative research.* New York: Aldine de Gruyter.

Kirk, J., & Miller, M.L. (1986). *Reliability and validity in qualitative research.* Newbury Park, CA: Sage.

Johnson, R.B. (1994). Qualitative research in education. *SRATE Journal, 4*(1), 3–7.

LeCompte, M.D., & Preissle, J. (1993). *Ethnography and qualitative design in educational research.* San Diego, CA: Academic Press.

Lincoln, Y.S., & Guba, E.G. (1985). *Naturalistic inquiry.* Beverly Hills, CA: Sage.

Maxwell, J.A. (1992). Understanding and validity in qualitative research. *Harvard Educational Review, 62*(3), 279–299.

Maxwell, J.A. (1996). *Qualitative research design.* Newbury Park, CA: Sage.

Okey, T.N., & Cusick, P.A. (1995). Dropping out: Another side of the story. *Educational Administration Quarterly, 31*(2), 244–267.

Smith, J.K. (1984). The problem of criteria for judging interpretive inquiry. *Educational Evaluation and Policy Analysis, 6,* 379–391.

Smith, J.K. (1986). Closing down the conversation: The end of the quantitative-qualitative debate among educational inquirers. *Educational Researcher, l5,* 12–32.

Stake, R.E. (1990). Situational context as influence on evaluation design and use. *Studies in Educational Evaluation, 16,* 231–246.

Strauss, A. (1995). Notes on the nature and development of general theories. *Qualitative Inquiry 1*(1), 7–18.

Strauss, A., & Corbin, J. (1990). *Basics of qualitative research: Grounded theory procedures and techniques.* Newbury Park, CA: Sage.

Yin, R.K. (1994). *Case study research: Design and methods.* Newbury Park: Sage.

Appendix C

Checklist of Evaluation Questions

Below are the evaluation questions presented in Chapters 2 through 12 of this book. You may find it helpful to duplicate this appendix for use when evaluating research reports. Limited permission to do so is given on page *ii* of this book. Keep in mind that your professor may require you to justify each of your responses.

Chapter 2 Evaluating Titles

____ 1. Is the title sufficiently specific?

____ 2. Does the title indicate the nature of the research without describing the results?

____ 3. Has the author avoided using a "yes–no" question as a title?

____ 4. If there is a main title and a subtitle, do both provide important information about the research?

____ 5. Are the primary variables referred to in the title?

____ 6. Does the title indicate what types of people participated?

____ 7. If the title implies causality, does the method of research justify it?

____ 8. Has the author avoided using jargon and acronyms that might be unknown to his or her audience?

____ 9. Overall, is the title effective and appropriate?

Chapter 3 Evaluating Abstracts

____ 1. Is the purpose of the study referred to or at least clearly implied?

____ 2. Does the abstract highlight the research methodology?

____ 3. Has the researcher omitted the titles of measures (except when these are the focus of the research)?

____ 4. Are the highlights of the results described?

____ 5. Has the researcher avoided making vague references to implications and future research directions?

____ 6. Overall, is the abstract effective and appropriate?

Chapter 4   Evaluating Introductions and Literature Reviews

____ 1. Does the researcher begin by identifying a specific problem area?

____ 2. Does the researcher establish the importance of the problem area?

____ 3. Is the introduction an essay that logically moves from topic to topic?

____ 4. Has the researcher provided conceptual definitions of key terms?

____ 5. Has the researcher indicated the basis for "factual" statements?

____ 6. Do the specific research purposes, questions, or hypotheses logically flow from the introductory material?

____ 7. Overall, is the introduction effective and appropriate?

Chapter 5   A Closer Look at Evaluating Literature Reviews

____ 1. If there is extensive literature on a topic, has the researcher been selective?

____ 2. Is the literature review critical?

____ 3. Is current research cited?

____ 4. Has the researcher distinguished between research, theory, and opinion?

____ 5. Overall, is the literature review portion of the introduction appropriate?

Chapter 6   Evaluating Samples When Researchers Generalize

____ 1. Was random sampling used?

____ 2. If random sampling was used, was it stratified?

____ 3. If the randomness of a sample is impaired by the refusal to participate by some of those selected, is the rate of participation reasonably high?

____ 4. If the randomness of a sample is impaired by the refusal to participate by some of those selected, is there reason to believe that the participants and nonparticipants are similar on relevant variables?

____ 5. If a sample from which a researcher wants to generalize was not selected at random, is it at least drawn from the target group for the generalization?

____ 6. If a sample from which a researcher wants to generalize was not selected at random, is it at least reasonably diverse?

____ 7. If a sample from which a researcher wants to generalize was not selected at random, does the researcher explicitly discuss this limitation?

____ 8. Has the author described relevant demographics of the sample?

____ 9. Is the overall size of the sample adequate?

____ 10. Is there a sufficient number of participants in each subgroup that is reported on separately?

____ 11. Has informed consent been obtained?

____ 12. Overall, is the sample appropriate for generalizing?

Chapter 7   Evaluating Samples When Researchers Do *Not* Generalize

____ 1. Has the researcher described the sample/population in sufficient detail?

____ 2. For a pilot study or developmental test of a theory, has the researcher used a sample with relevant demographics?

____ 3. Even if the purpose is not to generalize to a population, has the researcher used a sample of adequate size?

____ 4. If a purposive sample has been used, has the researcher indicated the basis for selecting individuals to include?

____ 5. If a population has been studied, has it been clearly identified and described?

____ 6. Has the researcher obtained informed consent?

____ 7. Overall, is the description of the sample adequate?

Chapter 8   Evaluating Instrumentation

____ 1. Have the actual items, questions, and/or directions (or, at least, a sample of them) been provided?

____ 2. Are any specialized response formats and/or restrictions described in detail?

____ 3. For published instruments, have sources where additional information can be obtained been cited?

____ 4. When delving into sensitive matters, is there reason to believe that accurate data were obtained?

____ 5. Have steps been taken to keep the instrumentation from obtruding on and changing any overt behaviors that were observed?

____ 6. If the collection and coding of observations is highly subjective, is there evidence that similar results would be obtained if another researcher used the same measurement techniques with the same group at the same time?

____ 7. If an instrument is designed to measure a single unitary trait, does it have adequate internal consistency?

____ 8. For stable traits, is there evidence of temporal stability?

____ 9. When appropriate, is there evidence of content validity?

___ 10. When appropriate, is there evidence of empirical validity?

___ 11. Is the instrumentation adequate in light of the research purpose?

___ 12. Overall, is the instrumentation adequate?

Chapter 9   Evaluating Experimental Procedures

____ 1. If two or more groups are compared, were individuals assigned at random to the groups?

____ 2. If two or more comparison groups were *not* formed at random, is there evidence that they were initially equal in important ways?

____ 3. If only a single participant or a single group is used, have the treatments been alternated?

____ 4. Are the treatments described in sufficient detail?

_____ 5. If the treatments were administered by people other than the researcher, were these people properly trained?

_____ 6. If the treatments were administered by people other than the researcher, was there a check to see if they administered the treatments properly?

_____ 7. If each treatment group had a different person administering a treatment, has the researcher tried to eliminate the "personal effect"?

_____ 8. Except for differences in the treatments, were all other conditions the same in the experimental and control groups?

_____ 9. If necessary, did the researchers disguise the purpose of the experiment from the participants?

_____ 10. Is the setting for the experiment "natural"?

_____ 11. Has the researcher used politically acceptable and ethical treatments?

_____ 12. Has the researcher distinguished between *random selection* and *random assignment*?

_____ 13. Overall, was the experiment properly conducted?

Chapter 10   Evaluating Results Sections

_____ 1. Is the results section a cohesive essay?

_____ 2. Does the researcher refer back to the research hypotheses, purposes, or questions originally stated in the introduction?

_____ 3. When there are a number of statistics, have they been presented in table form?

_____ 4. If there are tables, are their important aspects discussed in the narrative of the results section?

_____ 5. Have the researchers presented descriptive statistics before presenting the results of inferential tests?

_____ 6. If any differences are statistically significant and small, have the researchers noted that they are small?

_____ 7. Have appropriate statistics been selected?

____   8. Overall, is the presentation of the results adequate?

Chapter 11   Evaluating Discussion Sections

____   1. In long articles, do the researchers briefly summarize the purpose and results at the beginning of the discussion?

____   2. Do the researchers acknowledge their methodological limitations?

____   3. Are the results discussed in terms of the literature cited in the introduction?

____   4. Have the researchers avoided citing new references in the discussion?

____   5. Are specific implications discussed?

____   6. Are suggestions for future research specific?

____   7. Have the researchers distinguished between speculation and data-based conclusions?

____   8. Overall, is the discussion effective and appropriate?

Chapter 12   Putting It All Together

____   1. Have the researchers selected an important problem?

____   2. Were the researchers reflective?

____   3. Is the report cohesive?

____   4. Does the report extend the boundaries of our knowledge on a topic?

____   5. Are any major methodological flaws unavoidable or forgivable?

____   6. Is the research likely to inspire additional research?

____   7. Is the research likely to help in decision-making (either of a practical or theoretical nature)?

____   8. All things considered, is the report worthy of publication in an academic journal?

____   9. Would you be proud to have your name on the report as a coauthor?